Praise for *Emergence*

"The leaders winning right now aren't the ones with the best analysis. They're the ones who trusted their instincts and acted while others were still in the meeting. Jennifer Vessels brings twenty years of hard-won Silicon Valley and global transformation experience to a single, clear argument: in an age where AI makes expertise obsolete overnight, the competitive edge is human—purpose, curiosity, and the courage to act. *Emergence* shows you how—through her unique P.E.A.C.E. approach."

—Kimberly Mathiesen,
CEO of Hub Ocean, former GM of Microsoft Norway

"Jennifer Vessels is preparing us for a future that is coming at us faster than ever before. In *Emergence* she shows us why and offers a proven approach honed across Silicon Valley's transformations to navigate uncertainty and thrive with P.E.A.C.E."

—Bill Reichert,
General Partner of Pegasus Tech Ventures, Cofounder of Garage Technology Ventures and Startup World Cup

"This book is a timely reminder that the leaders who thrive in a rapidly changing world aren't the ones who know the most but the ones who have the courage to move first and to embrace the magic of the unknown. Jennifer Vessels, advisor for Fortune 100 transformations globally, shows us how to break free from outdated thinking."

—Simon Alexander Ong,
Business Strategist and author of Energize

"How do you lead when AI makes the old playbooks obsolete and change is accelerating faster than people can process it? Vessels provides a practical transformation approach that connects strategy, technology and human behavior. Every leader needs to read this book right now!"

—Suzanne McLarnon,
VP of MetLife, former director of Cisco Systems

"In an era where yesterday's competitive advantage becomes tomorrow's liability, *Emergence* delivers a much-needed wake-up call. Drawing on decades of success transforming corporate giants, Jennifer Vessels makes an impassioned and compelling case that survival now hinges not on size or legacy, but on the willingness to unlearn, adapt, and move with intention and intuition. This is a sharp, practical guide for leaders ready to trade the comfort of 'how we've always done it' for the momentum of 'what's next'."

—Michael Jenkins,
CEO of Expert Humans and partner of Future Work Forum

"In my work helping large organizations navigate technological change, one pattern keeps repeating: when uncertainty increases, leaders respond with more planning, more governance, and more control. Jennifer Vessels shows why that instinct is exactly what blinds us to what's emerging—and offers leaders a different way. It could not be more timely."

—Yngvar Ugland,
Innovation Fellow, DNB

EMERGENCE

EMERGENCE

How Leaders BREAK FREE from Outdated Thinking

JENNIFER VESSELS

WILEY

This edition first published 2027

Registered Offices
John Wiley & Sons, Inc., 111 River Street, Hoboken, NJ 07030, USA

John Wiley & Sons Ltd, New Era House, 8 Oldlands Way, Bognor Regis, West Sussex, PO22 9NQ, UK

John Wiley & Sons Singapore Pte. Ltd, 134 Jurong Gateway Road, #04-307H, Singapore 600134

For details of our global editorial offices, customer services, and more information about Wiley products visit us at www.wiley.com.

The manufacturer's authorized representative according to the EU General Product Safety Regulation is Wiley-VCH GmbH, Boschstr. 12, 69469 Weinheim, Germany, e-mail: Product_Safety@wiley.com.

Wiley also publishes its books in a variety of electronic formats and by print-on-demand. Some content that appears in standard print versions of this book may not be available in other formats.

Library of Congress Cataloging-in-Publication Data is Available:

ISBN 9781394439232 (Cloth)
ISBN 9781394439249 (ePub)
ISBN 9781394439256 (ePDF)

Cover Design and Image: Volodymyr Volianiuk
Author Photo: Courtesy of Jennifer Vessels

Set in 11/14.5 pts and Bembo Std by Straive, Chennai, India.

SKY10167629_090326

My father always believed I could. This book is proof he was right.

To Bear, Bobby, Jim, Katyanne, Leila, Madison, Maya, Mollie, Quinn, Payton, Sanna, Thao, Tim, Valerie—fourteen extraordinary people who emerged into my life and are my greatest inspiration.

You span from five years old to forty-two. You are Gen Z and Millennials and everything in between—navigators today into the future. Never stop emerging.

Contents

Prologue
The Woman on the Bridge

In May 1945, as the final battles of World War II raged across Europe, 19-year-old Marie Vessels stood at a bridge in Ampfing, Germany. Around her, German soldiers clutched their medals and weapons, some still believing they could hold back the advancing Allied forces.

Marie had spent six years watching war tear through her world. She'd hidden food for Jewish prisoners, knowing it could cost her life. She'd pedaled her bicycle across this very bridge daily, dodging Allied bombs to get to work. She'd listened to forbidden radio broadcasts and questioned what adults told her to accept without thinking.

Now, as tanks approached and townspeople panicked, Marie saw a choice. She could let fear decide what happened next. Or she could act on what she knew to be true.

"If these forces drove completely across Europe and are now here," she called out to the German soldiers blocking the bridge, "do you really think they will be stopped by your small attempt to block them with a pile of wood on the bridge?"

The German soldiers listened. They moved the debris.

When the Allied tanks slowed and soldiers climbed off to assess the situation, Marie raised both hands and shouted to the townspeople around her, "Put down your weapons then wave with both hands to show you are surrendering!"

To the advancing Allies, this young woman's voice carried something they hadn't heard in months of brutal fighting: surrender and calm. The Allied soldiers gratefully crossed the bridge in peace, moving the war closer to an end in this corner of the world.

Marie didn't know what would happen next. What she had was internal clarity about what mattered most: keeping people safe. No map. No plan. Just purpose and the courage to move. That's emergence.

Eighty years later, the bridge is different. The choice is the same.

Introduction

The Inflection Point Nobody Prepared You For

The storm has been building for years. Now it's emerging with full force.

Your biggest competitor isn't who you think it is. It's a 22-year-old with ChatGPT who never learned your industry's rulebook. They're delivering solutions while your strategic plans are being drafted. Building what's next while others protect what they built.

They navigate emergence naturally because they never knew anything else. They create without permission. They don't even know your rules exist.

We've reached an inflection point, a time of significant change.

Five massive forces, what I call *cyclones*, have been spinning independently for decades; they are Speed, Confidence, Meaning, Pressure, and what it means to be Human. Each one is reshaping how we work, lead, and create value. Early adopters felt these forces. Future-ready people adapted. But most treated each cyclone as separate: a climate challenge here, a technology investment there.

That separation just ended.

Over time, the five cyclones have become intertwined. Climate change is a result of capitalism. Technology advances drive redefinition of work. Shifting societal dynamics and geopolitics create entirely new conditions. The old playbooks are obsolete.

We're at a tipping point of change in which a new world is emerging. It can no longer be ignored, denied, or resisted. Markets are shifting before strategies can form. By the time expertise catches up, society, competition, and technology have moved again.

This is what I call Emergence—a new paradigm igniting change, shifting pillars of society, and creating the future.

Emergence doesn't reward those who know the most.
Emergence rewards those who move when nobody knows.

What Is Emergence?

Stop looking backwards, holding onto expectations, and waiting for things to settle down.

They won't.

Emergence is an unstoppable force driven by five cyclones spinning simultaneously, each strengthening the others, making yesterday's certainty today's obsolescence. Right now, these cyclones are colliding with unprecedented intensity. As their force increases, cracks will appear—creating space for a new world to emerge.

The five cyclones are:

- **Speed.** Technology is transforming entire industries overnight. Artificial intelligence (AI) is making expertise obsolete. Information is flooding every channel faster than meaning can be made. By the time you analyze the threat, it's already something else.
- **Confidence.** Every institution that provided stability is dissolving. Government, media, business integrity are all questioned more than followed. Authority no longer equals credibility. The structures that told us who we were have collapsed.
- **Meaning.** Traditional infrastructures—education, community, lifetime employment—are eroding without replacement. New generations are demanding purpose over paychecks, impact over income. The contract between work and worker is fundamentally changing.

- **Pressure.** Climate disruption is forcing infrastructure rethinking. Economic volatility is making planning impossible. Geopolitical instability is fracturing certainties. Every decision is carrying weight that compounds—supply chains, profits, survival itself.
- **Humanity.** If machines create, analyze, and deliver, what does being human mean now? As technology mimics productivity, creativity, and cognition, the question shifts from what can technology do to what makes people irreplaceable? Humanity itself is being redefined.

The inflection point is when these converging cyclones crescendo, creating space for the next paradigm to emerge. Those who are future-ready recognize this moment and navigate with confidence. Others freeze, waiting for external certainty that will never return.

This moment of Emergence is loaded with opportunity. While most leaders retreat to old playbooks, a small group recognizes what's possible when the skies clear, allowing the future to emerge.

The Gap Between Old Thinking and New Reality

Many leaders feel it: the exhaustion of working harder while falling further behind. First email changed communication. Then social media changed connection. Now AI changes everything. There is no return to what was.

People are afraid. Afraid of irrelevance as expertise expires. Afraid that someone half their age understands the future better than the entire C-suite. So leaders do what fear demands: they add complexity. Another framework. Another layer of approval. Another committee to study the committee's recommendations.

Fear isn't the problem. Paralysis is.

The leaders thriving at this inflection point aren't fearless. They've stopped letting fear make their decisions. They navigate with internal confidence when external certainty dissolves.

Your Head Knows Less Than Your Gut

In my work with Silicon Valley founders and chief executive officers (CEOs), this pattern shows up daily: the deals that feel right work, even when spreadsheets say they shouldn't. The hires who energize the room outperform the perfect résumés.

There's neuroscience behind this. Your gut has 500 million neurons processing information your conscious mind never sees. Your heart has 40,000 neurons sending more signals to your brain than receiving them.[1,2] Your body knows things your head hasn't figured out yet.

But most people have been conditioned to ignore these signals, to trust data over instinct. That worked when markets moved slowly enough for analysis to matter. Now, by the time you've analyzed, the opportunity's gone.

One person reminded me what it looks like to trust that inner knowing completely.

What Marie's Story Really Teaches

Marie's story from the prologue anchors this book not only because she's family—my uncle Heavrin's wife, my aunt by marriage—but she has been one of my greatest teachers through living example.

I learned about how she navigated impossible situations with clarity that came from absolute internal knowing. When she told me about the bridge decades ago, she wasn't sharing distant history. She was showing me what becomes possible when you stop waiting for certainty and act based on what you know inside.

Marie's story runs through every chapter of this book. You'll see why.

Why This, Why Now, Why You

The Industrial Age playbook many learned early in their career was not designed for today's environment. I have watched leaders at the world's biggest companies try to use 19th-century maps to navigate 21st-century storms. It fails every time. Emergence is not another framework to study. It's a navigation system to live by.

Silicon Valley is my homeland. Where I learn, grow, and return. Fertile ground for ideas, for exploration, for the future-ready mindset that drives everything here.

I am in the room when these transformations happen. I have spent decades working hands-on with leaders at Adobe, Google, Nvidia, and dozens of other companies as they navigate Emergence. I build navigation capability within leadership teams. I am in the trenches with them, helping them move confidently when the storm clouds impact people's ability to see the paths forward.

This book unveils the practical approach I use daily to deliver results with the world's most successful future-ready leaders.

While working across dozens of countries, I have learned something crucial: people in Silicon Valley operate differently. They are optimistic about the Emergence. Uncertainty is opportunity. "What does this make possible?" is how these future-ready people here breathe.

Two decades ago when I was based in England, the contrast between Silicon Valley and traditional mindsets was clear. Daily I heard "It is what it is. It has worked fine for centuries, why change" to my "It is great, let's make it better" and "What if?" questions. Both mindsets are valid. Only one allows for smooth navigation through today's emergence inflection point.

Release to Emerge

Emergence is possible when we let go—of expectations, societal rules, and external validation.

Personally, I learned this in 2015. I had the corner office, the gold lettering on the building, the income, the perfect life. Then my firm Next Step was hit with a brutal audit. During weeks of late nights with lawyers, two employees left threatening suits. My aunt's daughter died suddenly, and demanding clients were blowing up my phone during the funeral. Then the office rent tripled.

I looked at all of it and said: enough. All of the perks were no longer serving Next Step's purpose "to accelerate business success."

So, I let go of all the external trappings. What came next was not chaos. It was freedom. I reinvested in the right team, a non-traditional business model, new approaches. Today our work is way more exciting and impactful than I could ever have imagined a decade ago.

I've never followed a curated career plan. After college graduation I accepted a "safe" job as District Manager for Burger King. Then I received a call from an unknown tech company. Without question I chose the sales role in the technology company. This was an inflection point.

I learned by doing, exploring, pushing the boundaries. From selling systems to training sales teams and managing teams. While completing my MBA, I ran channel sales for a software scaleup in Mountain View until the CEO sold it out from under me and I nearly lost everything. Then I regained footing with Ungermann-Bass, where I led product marketing, enablement and sales operations.

At a critical inflection point within Ungermann-Bass, I relocated to Europe. From Brussels to England to Oslo, I built partners, teams, approaches and revenues.

Today, my purpose is clear: to have a lasting impact on the future—through empowering people. But that North Star has not always been in my sights. At seventeen my purpose was to pay rent. In my twenties it was to gain experience, learn and explore. Throughout my early career it crystalized and led me to establish Next Step in 2006.

Now as the winds shift, I ask: "how can this amplify my impact on people, business, clients?" When doors close, I ask: what does this free me to do? When the cyclones converge, I ask: "what matters most now?"

You don't need a better five-year plan. You need courage and confidence to navigate the next five days.

This book gives you three things:

- A clear view of what you're actually facing right now.
- The mindset to move forward without dragging old playbooks behind you.
- A practical path forward through P.E.A.C.E.

While my Silicon Valley roots and European base are fundamentally very different, I integrate the best of each culture into my work. Silicon Valley brings speed, risk tolerance, co-opetition (collaborating intensely while competing fiercely), and a bias toward action. Meet someone in a coffee queue, exchange ideas, have a partnership by afternoon.

Europe brings deep expertise, long-term thinking, and established relationships. Quality over speed. "It's well designed, tested, quality checked" meets "Let's see what happens."

My success delivering international growth comes from translating between them. European businesses need Silicon Valley's risk taking, exploration speed. Silicon Valley companies learn from Europeans' experienced perspectives. Leaders with a future-ready mindset don't just "go global." They recognize and leverage the value of all perspectives.

As the storm clouds swirl and the future emerges, the Industrial Age playbooks lack relevance. Navigation systems must be refined.

Moving into the Future with P.E.A.C.E.

I have built and battle-tested the P.E.A.C.E. methodology across two decades of delivering future-readiness for leaders, teams, people (see Figure I.1).

- **Purpose.** Your North Star that guides when maps dissolve. Clarity about what you are really trying to achieve and what matters when everything else shifts.
- **Exploration.** Discovering what's possible through questions, sampling new approaches. Finding paths by walking them.
- **Action.** Trying something new. Taking small steps, testing the ground and moving forward. Progress teaches faster than preparation.
- **Collaboration.** Engaging, asking questions, learning with team members, customers, co-creators from around the world. Building together what no one could create alone.
- **Empowerment.** Unleashing potential, not controlling output. Trusting people closest to problems. Encouraging, challenging and allowing growth.

As each chapter unfolds you will explore customer examples, gain insights, and learn practical ways you can navigate through the cyclones to reach your North Star with P.E.A.C.E.

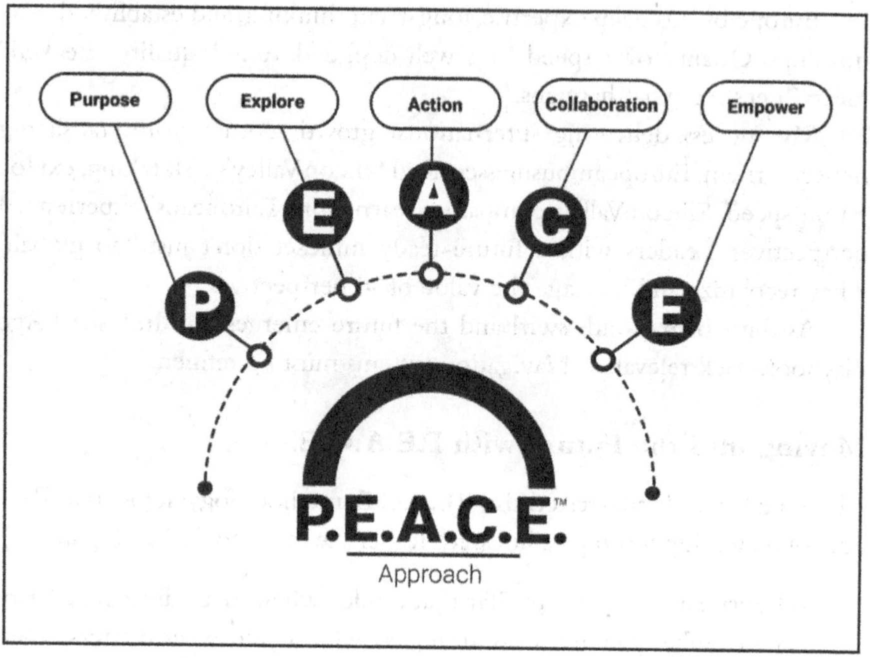

Figure I.1 The P.E.A.C.E. approach.

The Confidence That Comes from Within

When I work with CEOs facing Emergence, the first question I ask is never "What's your plan?" It's "What are you willing to stop pretending you know?" That admission is where real navigation begins.

External validation expires the moment conditions change. But internal confidence, the kind that comes from following your inner knowing, travels everywhere. You already have what you need. Your gut processes patterns faster than your head. Your intuition recognizes opportunities before logic labels them. Business schools can't teach this. Consultants can't package it. So they pretend it doesn't matter.

The proven P.E.A.C.E. approach is a way to reconnect with your own internal guidance. Five elements that work together. Purpose you feel in your bones. Exploration guided by curiosity. Action that emerges from inner knowing or intuition. Collaboration that forms naturally. Empowerment that releases what's already there.

Together, they spell P.E.A.C.E. Though as you'll discover, not the peaceful kind. This P.E.A.C.E. was born in Silicon Valley war rooms. It's strategic clarity under fire. It's how you move with purpose when you have no map.

It begins with understanding what the five cyclones colliding right now are about to teach everyone.

Who I Wrote This Book For

This book is for anyone navigating change, recognizing this inflection point or looking into the future. The individual contributor choosing how and where to work. The team lead deciding how to operate. The C-suite executive who feels the ground shifting. The entrepreneur evaluating paths to success. The conference organizer who wants to deliver impact, not another feel-good event.

You don't need a title to start. You need confidence in what you know inside. Marie was a teenager with a bicycle. Your competitors are twenty-somethings with nothing to lose. What they share: they acted on internal knowing while others waited for permission.

These pages hold the same stories, methods, and hard truths I deliver in keynotes and retreats for companies navigating leadership, digital transformation, and the future of work. It is the same practical emergence navigation I use with executives who need to move from fear to action in real time.

How This Book Is Structured

You are holding a compass, not a rulebook.

Rulebooks tell you what worked before. A compass orients you when conditions shift faster than any playbook can keep up with. That is the fundamental difference between the leadership tools that came before and what you will find in these pages.

The Emergence is organized in three parts, each building on the last. You can read it cover to cover, or use it as a field guide, returning to the sections most relevant to where you are right now. However you engage with it, know this: the goal is not comprehension. The goal is transformation in motion.

Part I: When the Map Disappears

Before you can move confidently through Emergence, you need to understand why the tools you have relied on are holding you back—and why that is not a failure of effort or intelligence.

Part I exposes the three forces that trap even the most capable people: the exhaustion of working harder inside a system built for a world that no longer exists (Chapter 1); the dangerous comfort of expertise in an era when deep knowledge can become a blindfold (Chapter 2); and the surprising truth that a new generation of natural navigators already holds the instincts many seasoned leaders are still trying to develop (Chapter 3).

This section will challenge you. It is meant to. You cannot build future-ready capability on top of obsolete assumptions. Part I clears the foundation.

Part II: Navigating with P.E.A.C.E.

This is the heart of the book—the practical navigation methodology I have built and refined across two decades of working inside the world's most complex organizations.

P.E.A.C.E. is not an acronym for a mindset. It is a sequential, actionable approach for moving confidently when certainty is gone. Purpose (Chapter 4) gives you the internal direction that replaces external maps. Exploration (Chapter 5) teaches bounded discovery—how to move into the unknown without losing your footing. Action (Chapter 6) breaks the paralysis loop that stops most leaders the moment conditions get uncomfortable. Collaboration (Chapter 7) shows how shared purpose multiplies what any individual can achieve alone. Empowerment (Chapter 8) releases the distributed capability already inside your teams and organization, waiting to be activated.

Each chapter includes real stories from Fortune 100 transformations, neuroscience-backed insights, and the approaches I use daily with clients. The P.E.A.C.E. methodology has been battle-tested in boardrooms and on the ground. It works when conditions are chaotic precisely because it was built for exactly that.

Part III: The Future Is an Invitation

Knowing what to do is only the beginning. Part III is about who you choose to become.

Chapter 9 builds the future-ready mindset that sustains your navigation capacity beyond any single crisis or disruption—the internal architecture that allows Emergence to become your competitive advantage. Chapter 10 issues the invitation directly: the future does not belong to the most experienced, the most credentialed, or the most resourced. It belongs to those who move when nobody knows.

The Epilogue and Appendix give you immediate tools—including a dedicated guide to navigating AI with P.E.A.C.E. so you can put this into practice the moment you close the book.

Throughout every chapter, Marie's story runs alongside the modern leaders, companies, and transformation moments you will encounter. She is there because she did something most of us spend our careers practicing: she acted with complete internal clarity inside complete external chaos.

That is Emergence. That is what you are here to discover.

Let's begin.

PART I

When the Map Disappears

> "In a time of drastic change it is the learners who inherit the future. The learned usually find themselves equipped to live in a world that no longer exists."
>
> —Eric Hoffer, *Reflections on the Human Condition* (1973)

In 2017, Netflix CEO Reed Hastings revealed something that made traditional executives uncomfortable: "I take pride in making as few decisions as possible, as opposed to making as many as possible."[1]

Many leaders hearing this felt their control instincts flare. Everything they'd been taught said the opposite, that leaders decide, others execute. More decisions meant more control. More control meant more success.

They were wrong.

Hastings understood what's now undeniable: when everything changes daily, centralized decision-making becomes organizational suicide. By the time information travels up, gets analyzed, receives approval, and travels back down, the opportunity is gone and the competitor has already shipped.

This is an early warning of Emergence, a continuous, interconnected evolution where everything affects everything else. Patterns form and dissolve faster than anyone can map them.

The Playbook That Built Everything

For more than a century, leadership followed a reliable script: analyze markets, build plans, execute with precision. Success came from knowing an industry, controlling variables, staying the course. This was the Industrial Age survival strategy. In stable markets with predictable competition, leaders who planned best and controlled most efficiently won. CEOs like Mike Lazaridis (BlackBerry) and John Antioco (Blockbuster) rose by mastering this system. Business schools taught it. Boards demanded it. It worked brilliantly, until it didn't.

The COVID pandemic accelerated what was already happening. As management consulting firm McKinsey reported: "Dramatic shifts are happening too quickly for companies to continue the traditional annual strategic-planning exercise. In fact, almost half the executives in our survey expect to implement a process that allows for faster iteration on their plans."[2]

This pace isn't temporary.

The Speed That Changed Everything

Research from McKinsey in 2024 highlighted the acceleration of technology. In just one year, organizations regularly using generative AI nearly doubled, rising from 33 percent to 65 percent. Broader AI adoption surged to 72 percent across various technologies after years of stalled growth.[3]

An estimated 90 percent of organizations are now undergoing some form of digital transformation,[4] with 93 percent[5] of workers across industries affirming that being digitally savvy is essential to performing well in their role.

Yet most still operate with Industrial Age thinking, adding AI to old processes rather than reimagining how work happens. The transformation is digital. The thinking remains analog.

At this inflection point, Emergence isn't approaching. It's here: perpetual, accelerating, irreversible. The five cyclones are colliding right now.

The Question Nobody Wants to Ask

How do you lead when guidebooks become obsolete before they're printed? When competitive advantage expires faster than you can document it? When the twenty-something with ChatGPT understands the future better than your strategy committee?

Stop planning and start thinking. You can't predict the future. Trust me, I've worked with companies in which people tried for decades. Instead, build the organizational capacity to respond to whatever emerges. Don't control change. Navigate through it.

The leaders thriving at this inflection point share something specific: they've stopped fighting uncertainty and started using it as raw material. They've shifted from leadership based on knowing to leadership based on navigating.

Three Uncomfortable Truths

In Chapters 1–3 you'll discover three truths that traditional leadership training never mentions.

First, working harder at what worked before guarantees exhaustion without success. The systems built for predictable markets become prisons in Emergence. In Chapter 1, you'll learn that every process you perfect will be perfecting your irrelevance.

Second, expertise (all that hard-won knowledge you've accumulated) will be your biggest barrier. In Emergence, not knowing becomes more powerful than false certainty. In Chapter 2, you'll learn that the illusion of expertise prevents the curiosity that creates breakthroughs.

Third, some people already navigate Emergence naturally. They're probably in your organization right now, driving you crazy with their "unrealistic" expectations and refusal to follow established patterns. In Chapter 3, you'll learn they're not the problem. They're the signal.

Be Future-Ready

Strategy evolves when you change how you think about uncertainty itself. That begins with understanding why the systems that brought you here can't take you forward.

1 Why Working Harder Isn't Working: The Inflection Point Where Old Systems Collapse

> "The significant problems we face cannot be solved at the same level of thinking we were at when we created them."
>
> —Albert Einstein, attributed (1946)

We've reached the inflection point where the Industrial Age systems that built our prosperity face conditions they were never designed for. The five cyclones of change that have been spinning independently for two decades are now colliding. *The forces themselves are not new. What is new is their convergence.*

The Industrial Age created real prosperity. Capitalism rewarded effort, funded growth, and built industries that employed millions. Clock in at nine, clock out at five. Paid by the hour, people learned that the more you work, the more you earn. That deal was honest and it worked. Follow the ladder from entry to executive. Master your craft through years of experience. Build expertise, defend territory, and protect knowledge. These weren't just workplace habits, they were survival strategies that worked for more than a century.

They led to the inherited prosperity: global corporations, stable careers, retirement systems, education structures that produced predictable results for predictable markets. These systems weren't wrong; they were brilliant for their time. Some elements still work perfectly for specific contexts: safety protocols, medical procedures, anywhere precision prevents catastrophe. But applying Industrial Age timing to emergence speed is like using a sundial to time Formula One races.

These systems were built for weather that no longer exists. The challenge isn't learning new systems, it's shifting the mindset that keeps us trapped in old ones.

Today, leaders exhaust themselves perfecting systems designed for stability in a world that rewards navigation. They're adding more process to manage chaos that feeds on process, seeking certainty in markets that punish those who wait for it.

The Industrial Age framework that built success (analyze, plan, execute, measure) assumes tomorrow resembles today. The brain prefers the familiar, even when it no longer serves. When things change faster than people can adjust, that preference locks them in place. And right now, AI is transforming industries in months while 20-year-olds with laptops outmaneuver billion-dollar corporations. The old framework isn't failing quietly. It's exhausting people still trying to make it work.

You can't fix a system by working harder when the system itself is the problem.

The hourly wage taught us time equals value, but now value happens in moments of insight. The expertise that took decades to build becomes liability when markets shift faster than experience accumulates. What makes people and leaders future-ready isn't abandoning expertise; it's balancing expertise with navigation capability. Being comfortable with expertise expiring. Recognizing that learning speed matters more than accumulated knowledge.

We're at the inflection point right now. Living in it. And it is moving faster than the Industrial Revolution, which took generations to unfold. Markets that took decades to form now reshape in months. Expertise that lasted careers now expires in years. The cyclones aren't just spinning faster; they're colliding with each other, amplifying disruption exponentially. This is perpetual emergence.

In August 2019, I stood in front of 120 people at the Executive Growth Alliance (EGA) Summit in Oslo. My opening statement made the room go quiet: "The world as we have known it—work, business, life, society—is not going to continue in this way. This will be the last time we are all together in a room like this."

Months later, COVID shut down the world. The theme for the EGA summit had been "Get Future Ready Now." We weren't predicting events. We were recognizing patterns.

During COVID, I thought that the paradigm had really shifted. I was wrong. That was just the warm-up.

Right now, what I saw coming in 2019 has arrived. The five cyclones I identified then were spinning independently. Now they're colliding. Climate intersects with capitalism. Technology collides with humanity. Work clashes with societal norms.

The inflection point wasn't a moment to pass through; it was the beginning of perpetual Emergence.

From Boxes to Flow

The Industrial Age organized everything into boxes. Job descriptions with rigid boundaries. Career paths following straight trajectories. Five-year plans. Expectations defining what "should" happen.

Boxes felt like structure, security, and control. They were designed for stability, when markets moved slowly, expertise lasted decades, and tomorrow reliably resembled today. In that world, boxes worked. They created predictability and enabled planning.

Business as usual is obsolete. And that's a *good* thing.

Marie understood this before she had words for it.

In May 1945, the German soldiers at the Ampfing bridge were operating entirely within their box. Their orders were clear. Their roles were defined. Their training said hold the position. Even as Allied tanks rolled across Europe and the evidence was overwhelming, they doubled down—more effort, more resistance, more commitment to a system that had already collapsed. Working harder inside a structure that had already failed them.

Marie had no box to work from. No authority, no rank, no script. What she had was clarity about what actually mattered—keeping people safe—and the willingness to move on that clarity when everyone around her was frozen by the rules of a world that no longer existed. She didn't fight the old structure. She simply stepped outside it and acted from purpose.

That is the shift this chapter is asking you to make. Not to abandon structure entirely, but to stop mistaking the box for the destination. The soldiers weren't bad people. They were good people trapped in obsolete thinking at exactly the moment when the world demanded something different.

Stop Defending the Bridge

The question isn't whether your current systems once worked. They did. The question is whether you're still defending the bridge.

The world that is emerging today doesn't fit in boxes.

Markets shift daily, and rigid job descriptions trap talent in obsolete roles. Five-year plans become anchors, not roadmaps. When reality contradicts what was planned, defending the box prevents seeing what's actually happening.

The emerging world operates differently; it's circular, fluid, adaptive. It's like water finding its path rather than rails forcing a direction. Purpose provides the destination, but the route adapts continuously based on what's actually happening, not what was planned.

This requires letting go. Of expectations about how things "should" unfold. Of plans that assume tomorrow will resemble today. Of key performance indicators (KPIs) measuring yesterday's priorities. Of boxes that worked brilliantly for weather that no longer exists.

Movement becomes more valuable than maps. Internal knowing becomes more reliable than external validation. Intuition becomes more trustworthy than "shoulds" from experts who navigated different conditions.

Emergence demands different structure. Fluid approaches instead of rigid boxes. Clear purpose with adaptive routes. Direction through alignment.

The shift isn't comfortable. Boxes feel safer even when they're failing. But organizations and individuals thriving in emergence share this pattern: they've stopped defending and trying to force reality into boxes and started flowing with what's actually emerging.

The Cyclones Colliding Right Now

The five cyclones aren't only metaphors. They're measurable forces that have been building for decades as the speed of innovation, pressure of capitalism, polarization of society, and distrust in institutions has accelerated. Today they are visibly colliding with each other (see Figure 1.1).

Each cyclone spinning alone forced leaders to adapt. The interactions between the cyclones create conditions the inherited systems were never built to handle.

It is through the collisions that Emergence occurs.

The Speed Cyclone

Fast is now the slowest that things will ever be. And at this inflection point, speed isn't just accelerating, it's colliding with the other cyclones. AI-driven speed meets work-life meaning. Technology acceleration hits geopolitical instability causing confidence to clash with humanity. If you're waiting for things to "settle down," you're navigating based on training (or a compass) from a different era.

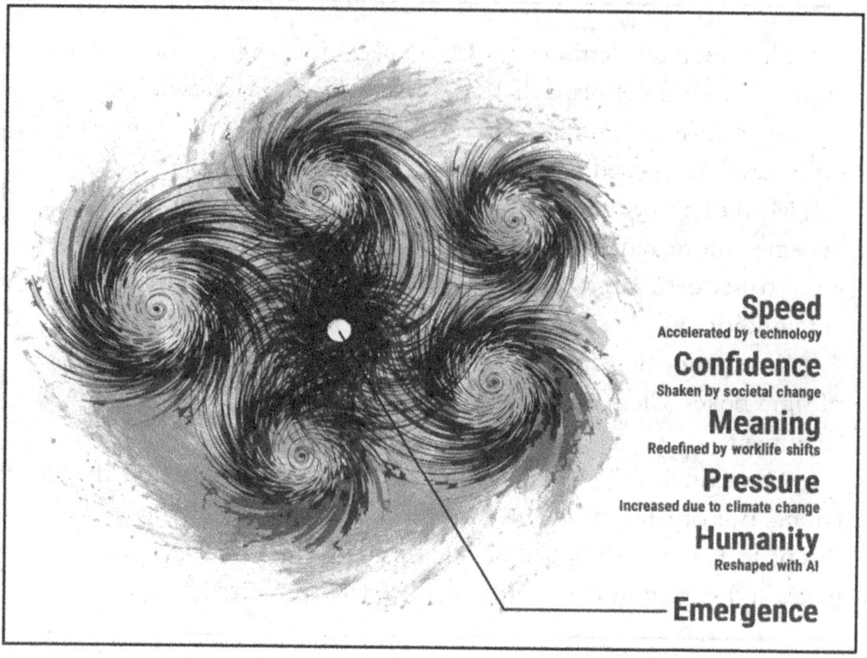

Figure 1.1 Cyclones of Emergence, a permanent state of change with five cycles of disruption spinning simultaneously and colliding with unprecedented intensity.

Technology rewrites entire industries before strategies can respond. AI makes knowledge and skills obsolete overnight. Information floods every channel with news, alerts, contradictions, and conspiracies until discernment becomes impossible. By the time you've analyzed the threat, it's already transformed into something else. The pace isn't just uncomfortable. It's existentially disorienting.

The following are not projections or predictions—they are the measurements of the storm already in motion:

- **Technology adoption acceleration.** The pace at which new technologies reach mass adoption has compressed from decades to months. The telephone required 75 years to reach 50 million users. Television took 13 years. The internet needed 4 years. ChatGPT reached 100 million users in 2 months after its November 2022 launch, one of the fastest consumer technology adoptions ever recorded.[1]

- **Corporate lifespan compression.** The average lifespan of S&P 500 companies has collapsed from 61 years in 1958 to roughly 20 years today, and is projected to shrink to just 12 years by 2027. At current churn rates, 75 percent of today's S&P 500 will be replaced by 2027.[2]
- **Knowledge doubling curve.** Buckminster Fuller observed that human knowledge doubled approximately every century until 1900. By 1945, it was doubling every 25 years. By 1982, every 12 to 13 months. IBM has projected that the growth of Internet of Things (IoT) data could push that rate to every 12 hours. The volume of information now produced makes traditional learning models obsolete.[3]

The Confidence Cyclone

In Industrial Age thinking, confidence is based on having the answer. Today confidence gives future-ready people the audacity to move when they have no clue what the answer is.

Every institution that provided stability is dissolving. Government, media, religion, and education are now questioned more than followed. Authority no longer equals credibility. Even identity markers such as gender, nationality, and career are fluid. The structures that told us who we were and how to succeed have collapsed, leaving people to navigate without clear guidance.

The data reveals just how far institutional foundations have shifted:

- **Institutional authority collapse.** Trust in government has plummeted from 77 percent in 1964 to 22 percent in 2024 in the United States. Media trust fell from 72 percent in 1976 to 31 percent in 2024. The restructuring is permanent. People seek truth and guidance elsewhere.[4]
- **The influence revolution.** More than half of US adults now get news from social media at least sometimes, while television preference has dropped to 34 percent. Nearly 70 percent of consumers trust product recommendations from influencers over direct brand messaging. A single TikTok creator can shift markets faster than million-dollar advertising campaigns.[5]

- **Decentralized authority rising.** Cryptocurrency users surpassed 420 million globally in 2023 and reached 562 million by 2024. Open-source contributions on GitHub approached 1 billion in 2024 alone, with 1.4 million first-time contributors joining the movement. Authority is shifting from centralized institutions to distributed networks.[6]

The Meaning Cyclone

People want their work to matter. That's the Meaning Cyclone.

Traditional meaning infrastructure that had given meaning to life including religion, community, and lifetime employment has been eroded without replacement. People quietly ask: what matters? What lasts? What guides me when external markers disappear? Meanwhile, new generations are searching for meaning in a world that stopped providing it.

When traditional meaning disappears, people don't wait—they act, and the data captures exactly how:

- **The great reprioritization.** Nearly 90 percent of younger professionals say having a sense of purpose is important to their overall job satisfaction. Around 40 percent have walked away from roles or employers that didn't align with their values. The median tenure for workers aged 25 to 34 is just 2.7 years, a 20-year low. Pay still matters and 80 percent of Gen Zs and Millennials report financial stress, but salary alone no longer holds people in place. When the work feels meaningless, they leave.[7]
- **Purpose-driven performance.** Purpose-aligned companies report 25 percent higher revenue and 22 percent higher pre-tax profit than peers without purpose metrics, according to the Center for Economic Performance's 2025 analysis of corporate performance data. Two-thirds of global consumers say they will pay more for sustainable brands, with Millennials leading at 73 percent. And 71 percent of consumers worldwide will buy or boycott a brand based on its position on social issues. Companies that ignore purpose don't just lose talent. They lose customers and investors.[8]

- **The engagement emergency.** Only 23 percent of employees reported being engaged at work globally in 2023, according to Gallup. That number dropped to 21 percent in 2024. Sixty-two percent are simply going through the motions, while 15 percent are actively working against their organizations. This disengagement costs $8.9 trillion annually in lost productivity, a massive 9 percent of global GDP. The antidote is clear: highly engaged employees are 87 percent more likely to stay with their organizations and deliver 23 percent higher profitability. And engagement rises when people connect their work to something that matters.[9]

The Pressure Cyclone

Pressure isn't a phase; it's the atmosphere. You don't manage it; you learn to breathe in it.

Climate disruption is forcing infrastructure rethinking. Economic volatility is making planning impossible. Geopolitical instability is fracturing long-standing certainties. Local systems absorbing global shocks in real time. Every decision carries weight that compounds and depends on navigating forces nobody fully understands.

The data reveals how multiple, interconnected pressures are converging at once:

- **Climate acceleration.** Climate-related disasters have nearly doubled since the 1980s, with floods alone more than doubling over two decades. In 2023, the warmest year on record, heatwaves, floods, and rapidly intensifying storms hit every inhabited continent. Weather emergencies force an average of 21.5 million people from their homes each year. Annual economic losses from extreme weather already average $143 billion and are accelerating. Supply chains, markets, and workforce availability are reshaping in real time.[10]
- **Economic volatility.** Global debt reached $318 trillion in 2024. Including all sectors, it stands at roughly 235 percent of GDP, well above pre-pandemic levels. Container shipping rates quadrupled between 2019 and 2022 as supply chain bottlenecks cascaded across industries. A handful of countries still face runaway inflation above

25 percent, and dozens more are managing rates well above their pre-pandemic norms. Traditional economic models cannot predict, much less control, these compound pressures. Organizations built for stability face markets defined by volatility.[11]

- **The produce-more trap.** Industrial Age capitalism created something extraordinary. It built the middle class. It funded innovation that transformed medicine, transportation, and communication. It lifted billions out of poverty and created opportunities that previous generations couldn't imagine. Paid by the hour, measured by production, valued by consumption. That system worked brilliantly for the world it was built for. But the race it created (produce more, earn more, buy more, discard, and repeat) now drives three compounding fractures: a distorted measure of human value, a widening divide between those who have and those who don't, and a planet unable to absorb what the cycle throws away. The system that brought us here needs to evolve, not disappear. Capitalism isn't the problem. The version of it we inherited is.[12]
- **Mental health crisis.** Anxiety and depression surged 25 percent globally in the first year of the pandemic alone, according to the World Health Organization. Seventy-six percent of employees say they experience burnout at least sometimes, with 28 percent reporting it "very often" or "always." Among US high school students, 40 percent report persistent sadness or hopelessness, up from 30 percent a decade ago. The source is friction between Industrial Age structures and people who navigate naturally. Force a navigator to act like a cog and they break. The cost shows up in decreased productivity, increased healthcare spending, and talent walking out the door. Leaders ignoring this lose their best people to competitors who get it.[13]

The Humanity Cyclone

What does it mean to be human when machines do your job better than you do?

As machines mimic skills and cognition, the question becomes: what does being human mean now? Humanity redefines itself while the infrastructure that previously defined it dissolves. Searching for meaning while algorithms optimize for engagement. Seeking connection while systems incentivize isolation.

The redefinition of humanity is not philosophical speculation—it is already being measured:

- **AI capability explosion.** AI surpassed human performance on reading comprehension benchmarks in 2017 and on English language understanding tasks by 2023. AI systems now outperform humans on specific, well-defined reasoning benchmarks. Goldman Sachs estimates 300 million jobs globally could be affected by automation, with most complemented rather than replaced. Seventy-two percent of companies used AI in at least one business function by 2024, up from 20 percent in 2017. The question is not whether AI will transform work but whether humans will define their value beyond tasks machines do better.[14]
- **The human premium.** Employers expect demand for creative thinking to grow 73 percent by 2027, according to the World Economic Forum. Analytical thinking ranks as the top skill employers seek, with emotional intelligence and empathy also rising in the rankings. As AI handles computation, human value shifts to capabilities machines cannot replicate: intuition, connection, and purpose.[15]
- **Identity revolution.** Baby boomers held an average of 12.9 jobs from age 18 to 58. Younger workers are on pace to exceed that number, with median tenure dropping to 3.9 years in 2024. More than a third of American adults maintain side hustles alongside primary employment. Work-life balance is being replaced by work-life integration, with purpose flowing through all activities rather than confined to separate compartments. Identity no longer comes from job title but from impact created.[16]
- **Connection paradox.** The average person can recognize about 1,500 faces, yet 61 percent of young adults reported serious loneliness in a 2021 Harvard survey. Young people aged 15 to 24 spend 70 percent less time with friends in person than they did two decades ago. We are more connected yet more isolated than ever. Organizations that create genuine human connection will attract talent fleeing digital exhaustion.[17]

The Pattern Is Clear

These are not independent forces. They are interconnected cyclones creating compound acceleration. Speed makes Confidence impossible to maintain through hierarchy. Confidence collapse makes Purpose and Meaning essential for alignment. Meaning or Purpose without addressing Pressure rings hollow. Pressure exposes what makes people Human. Human identity shifts accelerate Speed of change.

The convergence creates Emergence events. We've seen them: COVID, AI explosion, geopolitical landgrab, and whatever comes next. These aren't anomalies. They're the byproducts of colliding forces—and they're arriving faster and hitting harder.

Industrial Age thinking assumes these forces will stabilize, that we'll return to "normal." But the data shows the opposite. Speed is accelerating. The cyclones aren't temporary disruption. They're permanent reality.

The choice isn't whether to acknowledge these cyclones. They spin regardless. The choice is whether to navigate them with Industrial Age maps or with an emergence mindset that turns pressure into possibility.

These cyclones don't take turns. They spin simultaneously, each strengthening the others. Together, they've created perpetual motion where adaptation becomes the only continuity.

Leaders trained in the old system respond by adding complexity: another framework, another committee, another layer of process. Armor that becomes anchor. Complexity cannot solve what simplicity shows: weather cannot be controlled. It can only be navigated.

The Daily Mismatches

In Silicon Valley, where "question everything, build better" isn't a slogan but a survival strategy, these mismatches get amplified daily. Teams exhaust themselves on processes designed for predictable markets while competitors that started coding yesterday capture those same markets.

Most people know these patterns, whether CEO or janitor.

Leaders with an Industrial Age mindset track time in the office when valuable contributions happen in moments. The breakthrough during a walk. The solution in the shower. The 30-second connection that changes everything. Intuition, that inner knowing that signals opportunity before logic catches up, gets dismissed as "soft" when it's actually how navigation works.

Managers perfect five-year strategic documents based on what worked a decade ago while industries transform overnight. In the time it takes for a committee of 12 to align on the perfect approach, the competition has gained a million new users on the latest release.

People implement new systems while maintaining old thinking. The tools change and the exhaustion increases, because transformation starts in how people think, not what software they use.

These are mismatches between systems built for one world and people living in another.

When Success Becomes a Prison

In the introduction I told you how my business transformed nearly overnight. The corner office, the crisis, the choice to let go. What I didn't tell you is how long I ignored the signals.

For years, I could feel the gap between what looked successful from the outside and what felt right on the inside. The business grew. The team delivered great results. The clients kept calling. And every morning I had to convince myself that this was what I wanted. It felt more and more like a prison. Success that didn't fit.

The disruption was a welcome relief. Letting go of expectations, KPIs, and structures allowed me to create a more successful future-ready business that is thriving.

Every person reading this has their own version. The achievement that impresses others but drains you. The promotion that everyone celebrated except the person who got it. The corner office that felt smaller every year.

The Vocabulary of Obsolescence

The words we use shape reality. Every person wrestling with Emergence faces this: the inherited language assumes stability that no longer exists. The Industrial Age didn't just create organizational boxes, it required that bodies filled them. Each box had a title, a salary range, a reporting structure.

The bodies were interchangeable as long as they stayed within the lines. Later chapters explore why innovation today depends not on rigid boxes but on fluidity, curiosity, and the capacity to navigate emergence with intention.

Work-life balance assumes work and life are separate territories with clear borders—like the Flintstones clocking out at the quarry to go home. That made sense when work had a physical location and fixed hours. It doesn't match how purpose-driven people operate now.

The future doesn't include work/life separation. It evolves through purpose-driven people passionately working together, leveraging their curiosity, creativity, and intuition to co-create success. There is no concern of work-life balance as they integrate diverse perspectives moving toward their shared purpose.

The future-ready mindset: when building something that matters, the line between work and life disappears. Purpose makes it so. People collaborate with others who bring different perspectives. Creativity and intuition allow people to solve massive problems. Dedication comes naturally because purpose matters more than comfort.

Purposeful versus purposeless. Aligned versus misaligned.

The career ladder assumed vertical progression through predictable rungs. When roles transform faster than job descriptions update, when AI eliminates entire departments, where is the ladder? People now build portfolios, not careers. Best practices assumed what worked before would work again. In emergence, yesterday's best practice is today's constraint.

Change management assumes change is an event to manage between stable states. But when change is constant, what exactly gets managed? People don't need change management; they need confidence and tools to empower them to navigate through the fog when everything is in perpetual motion.

Human resources reduces people to assets to be allocated. When creativity, intuition, and purpose drive value, people are the entire game. Every person treated as a cog while being asked to innovate feels this contradiction.

The language trap is subtle. Using Industrial Age words for emergence realities, and wondering why nothing quite fits is like trying to describe the radiance of a color through a math formula. The vocabulary itself limits what's possible.

What Success Stories Had to Unlearn

Sometimes the biggest barrier to transformation is what needs unlearning.

Adobe, the company that revolutionized document and creative publication with Acrobat, Photoshop, and Creative Suites, faced an existential threat. The 2008 financial crisis exposed what had been building for years: the obsolesce of their business model of selling packaged enterprise software. The market shift had been underway since 2006. Customers postponed updates or moved to point solutions. The stock price fell to all-time low.

When I led Adobe through this transformation, the hardest part wasn't the technology shift from desktop to cloud, or the business model change from products to subscriptions. It was helping their leaders unlearn what had made them successful.

For decades, software was licensed for use on designated devices. This gave security, control, permanence. All in Adobe whose career had developed based on the premise of 18-month release cycles, needed to let go of the very rhythm that had underscored their careers and embrace continuous delivery without a finish line.

The launch celebrations and incentives had to go too. With a future-ready software-as-a-service (SaaS) model, quick wins replaced periodic big reveals.

In 500 BC Sun Tzu wrote that vulnerability emerges from strength. For decades, Adobe's strength was built on the predictability of 18-month release cycles. That same predictability became their greatest obstacle to success in 2008.

The unlearning was painful. But it created space for new approaches, revenue streams, and deeper customer loyalty to emerge.

What are you willing to unlearn?

The Generation That Never Knew Stability

People born after 1997 make up roughly 30 percent of the global population and growing.[18] They are the torch carriers of what is emerging. Not because they are smarter or braver. Because they never learned to expect stability in the first place. Climate crisis is just weather to them. Smartphones are oxygen. Real-time everything is how life works. They have never known stable career paths or pensions, so they do not miss them.

This isn't a forecast nor a trend report. It's reality.

Critics point to the mental health statistics of young people today as a sign of fragility. I'd call it honesty. The stress they feel is the same as others are experiencing, it's simply that people of Gen Z and Gen A admit it. They've also figured out that standing still is the most dangerous move. Instead, they choose a practical response to a world where traditional safety seems an illusion instead of a promise.

They build multiple revenue streams because reliance on one job, gig, or skill set is vulnerability. They create portfolios, not career paths, turning down promotions to join startups that align with their purpose. While committees debate implementing AI, they've already redesigned the workflow and delivered a solution.

Chapter 3 goes deeper into how these natural navigators operate, and what every leader can learn from them.

The future doesn't require permission. It requires action.

Your Turn: Future-Ready Reflection

These "Your Turn" questions aren't for workshop discussions or journal prompts. They're for every person ready to stop fighting change and start navigating into the future as it emerges.

About the systems:

- Which processes exist only because they've always existed?
- What are you measuring that no longer matters?
- Where is complexity masquerading as sophistication?

About your response:

- Where are you adding friction instead of flow?
- What are you protecting that's already gone?
- Which expertise has become your prison?

About the cyclones:

- Which cyclone are you exhausting yourself fighting?
- What would happen if you stopped resisting?
- Who in your organization already navigates these naturally?

About your readiness:

- What would you do if fear wasn't making the decision?
- What would you do differently if you accepted the old maps won't return?
- What needs to be unlearned before something new can emerge?
- Who around you (maybe younger, maybe quieter) already sees what you're missing?

The answers matter less than the asking, because in Emergence, the most dangerous words aren't "I don't know." They're "I already know."

The systems are broken. That's clear. But the real barrier to navigating emergence isn't in the structures. It's the battle between what's in your head and what's in your gut. And your head has been winning for too long.

And nowhere does "I already know" do more damage than in the minds of the people organizations trust most—their experts. Chapter 2 explores what happens when the very thing that made you successful becomes the obstacle standing between you and what's next. Because the battle between your head and your gut isn't just personal. It's structural. It's been engineered into every system, every promotion, every credential you've earned. The armor that protected you in the old world may be exactly what's slowing you down in this one.

2 Why Knowing More Isn't Helping: The Expertise Trap

"In the beginner's mind there are many possibilities, but in the expert's mind there are few."

—Shunryu Suzuki, *Zen Mind, Beginner's Mind* (1970)

Decades of building expertise create a particular kind of armor. The person with answers. The one others turn to for certainty. Every promotion, every recognition, every success reinforces the same message: knowing more means winning more. The Industrial Age built this worship of expertise deliberately. Factories needed specialists who knew one thing deeply. Corporations needed experts who owned their domain. The entire system, from education through retirement, rewarded accumulation of specialized knowledge. That made sense when markets moved slowly enough for knowledge to stay relevant.

Knowledge and credentials can feel like security. It's identity, value proposition, safety net. In stable markets, it was everything, the differentiator between success and failure, the barrier competitors couldn't cross, the value that justified the salary. Expertise took years to build and decades to master. It was supposed to be the thing that made someone irreplaceable.

Right now, as the five cyclones collide, that armor becomes a cage.

The Speed Cyclone makes knowledge obsolete before experts finish explaining it. What took 10 years to master gets automated in 10 months. The Confidence Cyclone means credentials matter less if someone cannot navigate uncertainty. The traditional résumé, the impressive degrees, the decades of experience—none of it means anything if someone freezes when the map disappears. The Meaning Cyclone shows that knowing facts matters less than understanding meaning. People do not want the expert answer anymore. They want solutions to specific challenges and human connection.

The more someone knows about how things have worked, the harder it often becomes to see what's happening now. Expertise can create blind spots exactly where vision is needed most. Every mastered pattern will prevent seeing new patterns emerging. Every successful framework becomes a filter that can screen out the very signals needed for navigation.

Think about Kodak's experts in chemical photography. They knew everything about film, the chemistry, the processing, the distribution. That expertise wasn't wrong. It was brilliant. It just became irrelevant when digital disrupted their industry. Their knowledge didn't transfer. Their expertise became the very thing that prevented them from seeing what was obvious to anyone not invested in film. The difference between being an expert and being future-ready is this: experts defend what they know. Future-ready leaders explore what they don't.

Breaking out requires critical thinking. Not the analytical kind taught in business school. The kind that questions expertise. That asks "What if I am wrong?" before asking "How can I prove I am right?" The kind that values learning over being right.

While leading Silicon Valley startups' growth into Europe, I have seen this pattern frequently. Executives with 30 years of experience after graduating from top schools are displaced by 25-year-olds who dropped out of college but have already sold their first startup. Experience in the wrong context becomes liability. The expert often sees what they expect to see. The future-ready navigator sees what is actually there.

The expert says, "This is how it works," while the future-ready mindset questions, "What are we trying to achieve and how might this help reach that goal?"

At today's inflection point, experience built in stable conditions can become a constraint in emerging ones.

What got you here can't get you there.

What got you here won't get you there. It's the very thing holding you back.

The expert keeps stacking credentials to quiet the nagging truth that credentials stopped mattering. More certifications. More frameworks. More methodologies. Piling weight onto armor that's already dragging them under.

The illusion of knowing runs deeper than thought. Identity built on being the one who knows. Value chained to having answers. Saying "I don't know" doesn't feel like honesty—it feels like annihilation.

Fear takes over from there. Without answers, you have no value. So you do what feels safe: accumulate more. More complexity, more layers, anything to avoid the raw vulnerability of not knowing. But in emergence, every layer you add pulls you down faster.

So the performance grinds on. Projecting confidence while feeling lost. Stacking complexity to mask confusion. Speaking louder to drown out doubt.

Meanwhile, someone without the burden of expertise is building the future, because they're not trapped by what they know.

When Your Brain Blocks Progress

In emergence, biology becomes the biggest barrier. This resistance isn't a character flaw. It's neuroscience fighting what the body perceives as threat.

Deep in the brain, the substantia nigra (that ancient region managing reward and habit) craves familiar patterns (see Figure 2.1). It literally rewards humans with dopamine for recognizing what they've seen before. Every time existing knowledge applies successfully, the brain celebrates. The biological programming seeks the comfort of knowing.

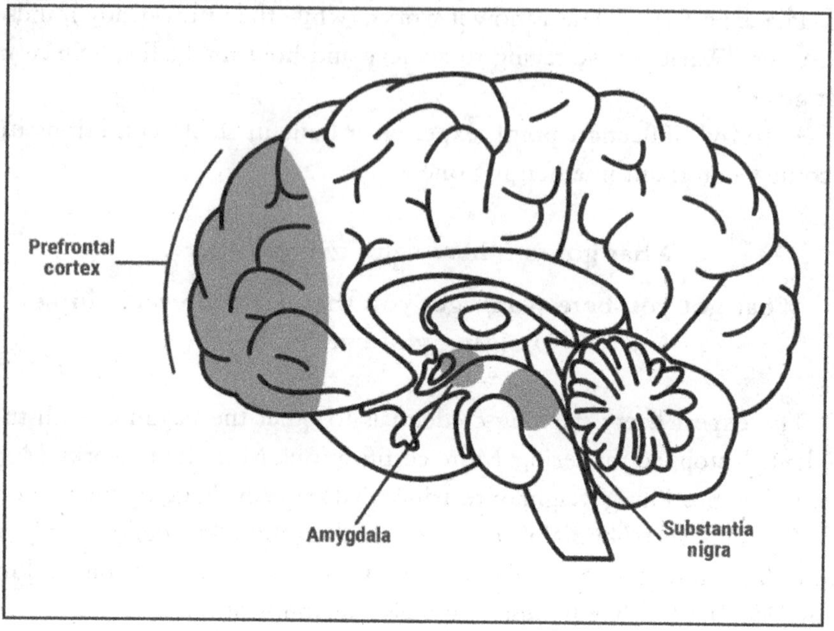

Figure 2.1 The neuroscience of emergence (shaded areas are for illustrative purposes and not exact scientific representations).

Meanwhile, uncertainty triggers the amygdala faster than conscious thought. Before anyone can think "I don't know," the body is already in threat mode. Heart rate increases. Stress hormones flood. The prefrontal cortex that can navigate creatively through uncertainty gets hijacked by the part screaming "danger!"

The response varies but falls into three patterns: fight looks like aggressive defense of old systems, attacking new ideas, dismissing different approaches. Flight looks like avoiding decisions, endless analysis, hiding behind process. Freeze looks like paralysis, inability to choose, waiting for someone else to move first.

Watch any person or organization facing emergence and you'll see all three. The executive fighting to preserve their KPIs. The manager organizing endless meetings. The team frozen, waiting for perfect clarity that won't come. All biological responses. Your brain reads emergence as danger because it can't predict what happens next. So it defaults to fight, flight, or freeze.

The problem is, emergence isn't a threat. It's a shift. And you can't fight, flee, or freeze your way through a shift.

Conscious thought is "expensive." The prefrontal cortex where creativity, critical thinking, and decision-making happen uses 20 percent of the body's energy while representing only 2 percent of body mass. That's why uncertainty exhausts us neurologically. The brain burns massive energy trying to process what it can't categorize.

Think of your brain's energy budget like a phone battery. The substantia nigra runs autopilot mode, low energy, high efficiency. The prefrontal cortex runs analytical mode, high energy, low capacity. In emergence, leaders who try to consciously analyze everything drain their cognitive batteries by noon. Those who develop autopilot for routine decisions preserve brain energy for what actually demands—conscious thought.

The brain isn't built for disruption. It's built for repetition.

This made perfect evolutionary sense. For 300,000 years, human brains evolved to reward pattern recognition and punish uncertainty. Neural wiring that kept our ancestors alive in stable environments. That same wiring now works against us in constant emergence. Our ancestors who recognized familiar threats and responded with learned patterns survived. Those who stopped to contemplate novel approaches to saber-toothed tigers didn't survive long enough to pass on their genes.[1]

Emergence isn't the "tiger" people think it is.

And Emergence creates constant biological alarm. Every change triggers stress hormones. Every uncertainty floods cortisol. Every pivot demands adaptation energy. The human body can handle acute stress. The tiger appears, you respond, it's over. But chronic uncertainty creates chronic biological cost. Fatigue that sleep doesn't fix. Exhaustion that vacation doesn't cure. Depletion at the cellular level from being constantly "on."

Change fatigue isn't psychological weakness. It's biological reality. The body treating every market shift like a survival threat. Every reorganization like a predator. Every technology change like danger. No wonder people are exhausted. They're running emergency systems continuously.

The Humanity Cyclone drives questions biology isn't built to process: what does being human mean when machines think? The Meaning

Cyclone demands navigation by purpose, not survival. The Pressure Cyclone compounds complexity beyond what pattern recognition can handle. Brains wired for stable environments where expertise meant survival now fight against the very adaptation emergence requires.

The people most confident in their knowledge are often the least capable of learning.

The more successful someone has been, the stronger these neural pathways. Every time expertise worked, the brain carved those grooves deeper. Now those grooves are ruts. Biology rewards applying old patterns to new problems, even as those patterns guarantee failure. Fear drives this even deeper. Fear of not knowing. Fear of losing value. Fear that without expertise, there's nothing left. So people accumulate more credentials, more certifications, more knowledge, thinking it will finally provide security. But in emergence, more weight just makes drowning happen faster.

But our brain is only a portion of the human body. Our "gut" is comprised of 500 million neurons—the enteric nervous system—processing information that the conscious mind never sees.

That intuition dismissed as "soft"? It's identifying patterns too complex for conscious analysis. That "feeling" about a decision? It's non-conscious intelligence navigating faster than thought. But expertise drowns out these signals. The more someone knows, the less they recognize what they feel. And in emergence, feeling will be more valuable than knowing.

The question shifts from "What should I do?" to "Who can I be?" That's when internal knowledge becomes identity. This circumvents the brain's tendency to avoid change by building a fortress around the familiar and calling it truth.

The prefrontal cortex is also the slowest and most energy-intensive part of the brain. Research shows most adults spend only a fraction of their mental time there, defaulting instead to faster and automatic processing systems rooted in habit and emotion. Children engage the prefrontal cortex naturally when exploring and questioning. But adults learn to conserve that expensive energy, relying on patterns even when patterns don't work.

Efficiency has become a trap. The brain rewards pattern recognition with dopamine and punishes uncertainty with stress hormones. Mental shortcuts save energy but reduce possibility. Familiar patterns feel safer but blind people to what is emerging.[2] The boxes people get sorted into (the visionary, the operator, the tech expert) become mental shortcuts. The Industrial Age mindset loves boxes. What begins as context turns into constraint. Boxes are built for storage, not expansion.

Education That Creates Fragility

From birth to age five, the prefrontal cortex is wide open. Children navigate by intuition, learn through curiosity, see possibility everywhere.

Then school arrives, and with it, the box. Sit still, follow instructions, compete with peers, memorize answers, repeat on command. What institutions call "preparation."

Preparation for what? To follow rules in a world that rewards rule-breakers? To wait for instructions in markets that move faster than committees? To climb ladders that no longer exist?

The education system is actively producing fragility. Churning out people who can't make decisions without rubrics. Who panic when paths aren't clear. Who are told to think critically but are penalized when they actually do.

This system built people who could thrive in stable conditions. People who can memorize processes, follow procedures, execute predictably. Those capabilities still matter. But Emergence also needs navigators. The system doesn't build those. It's still handing out gold stars for compliance while the world rewards those who color outside the lines.

Education taught people to seek the expert with answers. But in emergence, experts are often the last to see change coming. Their identity depends on current patterns persisting. The expert on traditional retail didn't predict e-commerce. The expert on hotel management didn't anticipate Airbnb.

Often when working with senior executives in traditional companies, I see the pattern. The more degrees on the wall, the harder it becomes for someone to say "I don't know." They've been promoted for having answers. Now emergence rewards those confident without them.

The educational system doesn't teach wrong things. It teaches the wrong relationship with knowledge. Every red mark says ignorance is failure. Every test exposes uncertainty as a weakness. People have learned to hide not knowing, fake certainty, project expertise.

Generations learned that admission of ignorance is a confession of inadequacy. That intuition is less valuable than instruction. That inner knowing matters less than approved answers.

It has been done with good intentions. That doesn't make it less harmful.

The generation now leading others into emergence was rewarded for the behaviors that emergence now punishes—gaining certainty over curiosity, answers over exploration, following the approved path over the instinctive one.

The world changed. The education system didn't. And its wiring travels with every leader who sat in those classrooms: waiting for permission instead of taking initiative, reaching for credentials instead of trusting judgment, adding complexity where simplicity would serve. They were taught to perform competence. Emergence demands something harder—the willingness to not yet know.

When "I Don't Know" Becomes Power

I learned early how powerful neural programming can be. My childhood wasn't what you'd call warm or easy. I discovered it was safer to stay quiet, to avoid standing out. I got good at sensing rather than speaking, reading the room, adjusting, fitting into whatever was expected. It kept me safe. But it also taught me to seek certainty and approval instead of having confidence in my own sense of things. That early wiring stayed with me for a long time. Until I realized I was building a career on the same instincts that once kept me small.

In 2009, Adobe's CEO Shantanu Narayen said something that would have ended most executive careers. What matters here is what he didn't say: "I already know."

In Emergence, the most dangerous words aren't "I don't know." They're "I already know."

Admitting uncertainty creates space for discovery. Pretending to know closes possibilities. Leaders in Adobe could not analyze their way into transformation. They had to navigate through it. They kept their "enabling creativity" purpose clear even when they did not know how to get there. The destination mattered more than the map.

There's tremendous freedom in admitting "I don't know." Not knowing doesn't make someone weak. It makes them open to possibilities. Open to learning, to adapting, to seeing clearly.

One of the most powerful phrases I use in my work is: it depends. I don't say it to dodge questions. I say it because context matters. What's right for one moment, team, or market will be entirely wrong for another. This is a common Silicon Valley statement and demonstrates a future-ready mindset.

"It depends" is a discipline. It forces examination of context rather than applying universal solutions. It stops the pretense that leadership is plug-and-play, that expertise transfers perfectly across situations.

"I don't know" is the beginning of innovation, not the end of credibility. Every startup begins with founders admitting they don't know if their idea will work. Every breakthrough starts with someone saying "What if?" instead of "I know that."

The comfort with not knowing creates what expertise can't: curiosity, experimentation, adaptation. When someone knows, they stop looking. When they don't know, they stay alert. In emergence, alert beats expert every time.

I've lived inside that tension. I grew up valuing knowing. I built a career on being the person with the answers. The questions got harder. The pace got faster. And the answers I'd relied on stopped being enough.

That's when "I don't know" stopped being a weakness and became my sharpest tool. Not as surrender. As navigation. When I stopped needing to be the smartest person in the room, I started seeing what the smartest person in the room always misses.

My transformation required something most people avoid: reflection that makes mindset visible. Active reflection. Sensing internal defaults. Noticing the stories running in the background. The assumptions going unquestioned. The fears making decisions. The goal is internal clarity about what is driving behavior.

In late January 2020, I flew to Europe for a five-week business trip. By March, borders had closed. Flights cancelled. I didn't leave Norway for two years.

Everyone kept asking: "When are you going home?"

I didn't have an answer. No plan. No map for navigating a global pandemic. No certainty about when, or if, I'd get back to the Bay Area.

No clue. No fear.

I had no fear. What I felt instead was clarity. The scaffolding of certainty that people relied on, the five-year plans, the performance reviews, the predictable routines, had fallen away. And I was fine. Better than fine. I had been navigating without those maps for years. COVID just made the rest of the world join me.

I expanded Next Step's client base in Europe. I launched Executive Growth Circles on a digital platform within weeks of lockdown. I chose to make Norway my base going forward. Not because I was stuck. Because it made sense. Purpose, intuition, serendipity. The same three forces that had driven every major decision in my life.

What began as disruption became discovery. Not because the rules fell away, but because I'd already learned to navigate without them.

I wrote this book because I have lived what happens when maps disappear and people keep moving anyway. When systems collapse and the discovery is that it is fine without them. When people ask "what do we do?" and the answer is "navigate with intuition."

"I Don't Know" Is Not Weakness—It's the Starting Line

I have been empowering leaders navigation of Emergence for more than three decades. COVID made it essential. And now the world has caught up.

"I do not know" is acknowledgment of reality. Nobody knows how AI will reshape work or which industries will exist in five years. Pretending to have these answers exhausts people.

Mo Gawdat, former chief business officer at Google X, shows us something profound: suffering comes from expecting external clarity and not finding it.[3] When predictability is treated as a promise, its absence feels like failure.

> The power in "I do not know" comes from what follows: "but let us find out." That curiosity, that willingness to explore without guarantees, that comfort with navigation over knowledge is what emergence rewards. The expert defends what they know. The navigator discovers what they don't.

The Inner Knowing That Actually Works

While your head accumulates expertise, your gut processes Emergence.

That "feeling" about a deal that creates hesitation despite perfect spreadsheets is millions of neurons processing patterns too complex for conscious analysis. That intuition about a hire that overrides the impressive résumé is embodied intelligence detecting what expertise misses. That inner knowing that whispers "something's shifting" while data says everything's stable is the navigation emergence requires.

But most people have been taught to ignore these signs. To trust external validation over internal knowing. To choose data over instinct, analysis over intuition, expertise over feeling. The louder the external noise, the quieter that inner voice becomes.

Fear drowns out intuition. Both speak through the body with increased heart rate, gut feelings, physical tension. But fear screams while intuition whispers. Fear says "danger, retreat, protect." Intuition says "notice, explore, move." Learning to distinguish between biological alarm and navigational guidance will be the most important capability in emergence.

Markets move faster than analysis can track. By the time someone has studied the opportunity, it's transformed. But intuition processes in parallel, not sequence. It recognizes patterns instantly, before conscious minds can label them. In emergence, that speed matters more than accuracy. Better to be approximately right instantly than precisely wrong eventually.

Confidence isn't knowing what will work.
It's knowing you'll figure it out.

Marie understood this at thirteen. Working at the German Air Force base, surrounded by adults who knew the rules, knew the hierarchy, knew what was expected, she listened to forbidden radio broadcasts instead. The adults around her had expertise in how the world worked. Marie had something more useful: the willingness to question what she was told. She didn't know what would happen. She knew what felt true. That inner knowing kept her alive for six years of occupation while people with far more expertise followed orders into catastrophe.

When change happens, the human body naturally reacts. There's a progression that most people miss (see Figure 2.2). **Instinct** is your body's immediate response driven by the amygdala in our brain. It quickly fires creating the flinch, the gut clench, the sudden alertness. It's millions of years of evolution keeping you alive.

Future-ready navigators recognize this and avoid immediate reaction. By stepping back, taking a deep breath they tap into **Intuition**. By going beyond instinct deeper into the unconscious mind, they can process patterns too complex for conscious analysis.

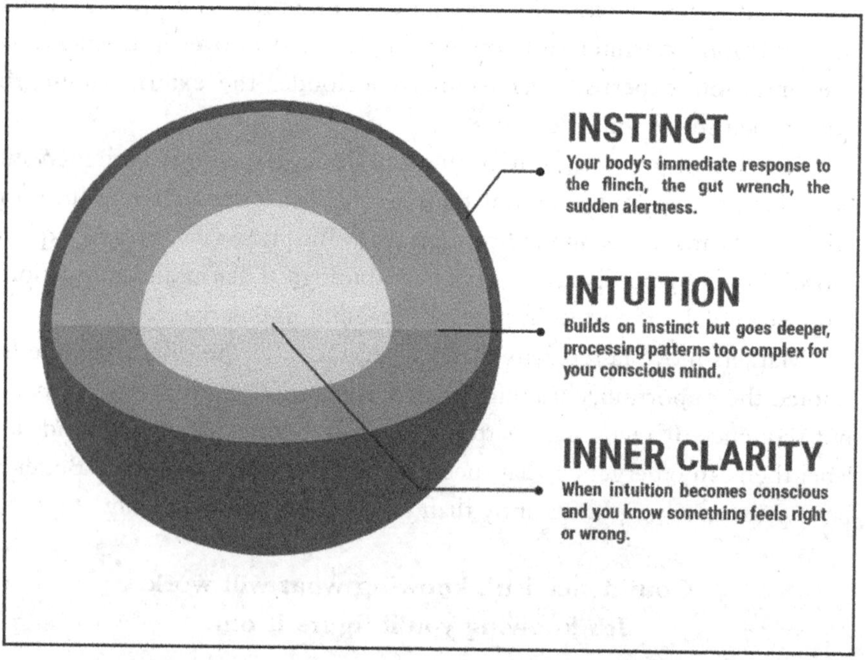

Figure 2.2 The movement toward inner clarity and emergence.

Most people stop at instinct, they feel something and either obey it (fear) or ignore it (dismissal). But those who are truly ready for the future have learned to go deeper. They notice instinct: "My body is responding." They explore intuition: "What patterns am I sensing?" "Where have I experienced this before?" and "What might I learn from it?" This provides inner clarity, supporting movement from reaction and reflection to response (see Figure 2.3).

Leaders such as Narayen, who guided Adobe through transition from software to service, go beyond intuition to gain inner clarity—real conviction to move forward based on their experience, knowledge, and internal sense of direction.

Inner clarity is when intuition becomes conscious and you know something feels right or wrong, even if you can't fully explain it.

When faced with Emergence, recognize the instinctual reaction, tap into intuition for insights then go deep as you reach for inner clarity: "What is this telling me? What does this mean about my alignment with purpose?"

In Emergence, this progression happens fast. A founder instinctively recoils from an investor offer. Their intuition says something's misaligned. Inner clarity shows the investor wants an exit that betrays the company's purpose. The whole progression takes seconds, but each level adds intelligence.

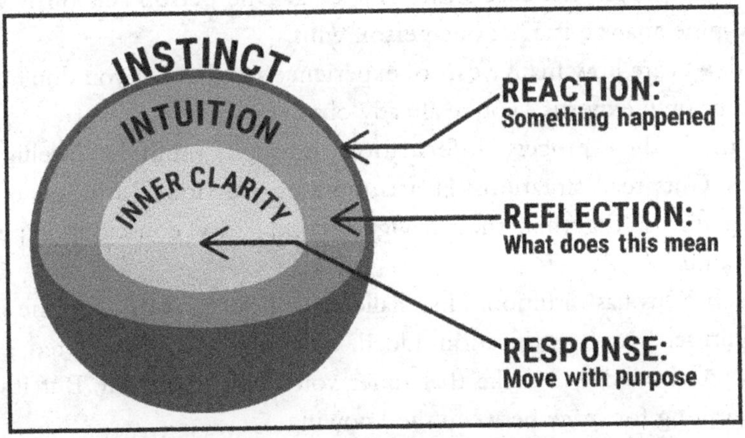

Figure 2.3 Future-ready leaders move from reaction to reflection.

The exhaustion many feel comes from stopping at instinct and living in constant biological alarm, rather than developing through intuition to inner clarity. They're stuck in reaction instead of reaching response. But when you develop from instinct through intuition to inner clarity, navigation becomes possible.

Aligning with purpose demands navigation by meaning, not metrics. Spreadsheets cannot calculate purpose. Analysis cannot quantify meaning. Intuition recognizes alignment instantly. The pull that says "this way" even when logic says "impossible." That energized feeling when work connects to something deeper. The internal compass that points toward purpose even when external maps dissolve.

In Silicon Valley, the most successful people have confidence in gut over head. They make billion-dollar decisions based on intuition, then use data to support it. They have learned that inner knowing navigates better than external expertise.

**Expertise is knowing everything about yesterday.
Navigation is figuring out tomorrow.**

Knowledge today is information. Data has limited value by itself. The question isn't what you know, it's what you'll DO with what you know. A hundred people can access the same data. One person acts on it while ninety-nine analyze it. That one person wins.

I don't care how many years of experience you have. If you don't question your own expertise, you're already obsolete.

Our bodies process information through multiple intelligence centers. Guts read situations. Hearts sense connections. Intuition recognizes patterns. Together, they navigate complexity conscious expertise can't handle.

Each of us has intuition. The challenge is hearing it through the noise of expertise. Every certification added, every framework mastered, every success celebrated will make that inner voice harder to hear. But it's still there, waiting for space between the knowing.

Your Turn: Inner Clarity Reflection

Something has to go. What follows might surprise you:

About expertise:

- What knowledge has become prison rather than power?
- How does being the expert prevent curiosity?
- Which credentials matter less than people pretend?

About biology:

- When does the body signal threat that's actually opportunity?
- Where does comfort-seeking prevent growth?
- What patterns get clung to that no longer serve?

About learning:

- What would be worth exploring without needing to be the expert?
- Where is certainty being performed instead of curiosity admitted?
- Who nearby models comfort with not knowing?

About intuition:

- What is your gut saying that your head won't accept?
- Where does inner knowing conflict with external expertise?
- When was "feeling" trusted over "analysis"? And what happened?

The answers don't matter as much as the admission: nobody has them all. And that not knowing isn't weakness. It's the beginning of navigation. The most powerful shift isn't from not knowing to knowing. It's from needing answers to becoming curious about questions. Curiosity navigates where expertise hits walls.

The systems are no longer working. Chapter 1 revealed that. It's becoming clear that expertise can't fix them. But there's a generation moving through every organization that navigates this naturally, without the burden of expertise or the weight of knowing. Younger professionals have never expected stability, so uncertainty doesn't paralyze them. They build portfolios instead of climbing ladders. They create their own authority because no institution ever promised them any.

Marie lived this. She navigated a bridge in wartime the way future-ready people navigate business today: by following what she felt when what she knew wasn't enough.

In the next chapter, meet the people doing this right now. They're not special. They're just not trapped by what they know.

3 Why Some People Already Get It: The Natural Navigators

> "We will experience more change this coming decade than we have in the entire past century."
>
> —Peter Diamandis, co-founder of Singularity University

There's a pattern emerging in every organization, visible to anyone willing to see it. Some leaders freeze. Others flourish.

What distinguishes the future-ready navigators isn't just mindset, experience, and the confidence to explore; it's inner strength. The kind that comes from trusting yourself when maps disappear. The kind that doesn't require external validation to move forward. At this inflection point, some people navigate the colliding cyclones without exhaustion. They surf uncertainty, create momentum, move by instinct. It's not that they don't struggle; they do. But they have grit that goes beyond traditional definitions. Not endurance for endurance's sake, but the determination to keep navigating toward purpose no matter how often the route changes.

My aunt Marie was the first natural navigator I ever knew. No training. No title. No authority. A young girl riding a bicycle through occupied territory, reading situations faster than the adults around her, acting on instinct when expertise said freeze. Everything this chapter describes about natural navigators, she lived before any of us had language for it.

These navigators span ages. A 23-year-old who's never known stable ground. But also the 60-year-old CEO who disbanded annual planning for quarterly experiments. The 45-year-old director who turned their department into a learning lab. The 30-something founder who pivoted three times before finding alignment.

They feel fear; everyone does. But they don't let fear mean stop. For them, fear points to transition, not threat. Their gut reads situations differently than their prefrontal cortex. Protective fear says stop, expansion fear says go. This neurological distinction is what makes them future-ready. The same uncertainty that triggers panic in those expecting stability triggers curiosity in those expecting emergence. Not fearlessness but a different relationship with fear. And they're closer than you think.

There's a cohort moving through your organization who already navigate this inflection point naturally. They've never known stability, so they don't wait for it. They learned to create in uncertainty because uncertainty is all they've experienced. They operate with a clarity that looks like confidence, and it is.

You might call them pushy. Unrealistic. Naive.

What if they simply recognize what you're still learning? They make decisions based on what energizes them because they watched their parents or colleagues burn out chasing metrics that didn't matter. They evaluate opportunities through resonance because they've seen prestigious careers evaporate overnight. They trust their inner knowing because they learned early that external validation expires.

They're not ignoring your experience. They're integrating it with their lived experience of constant change. The shortcuts you can't see? They're navigation paths formed by growing up at this inflection point.

Watch them work. When something feels misaligned, they pivot immediately. When opportunity resonates, they move without waiting for permission. They're not reckless. The Gen Zs, in particular, are fluent in a language you're still learning: the language of emergence.

You may see headlines about Gen Z's high levels of anxiety. Do not mistake their physiological stress for lack of courage. They aren't anxious because they're afraid of the future. They're anxious because they're the first generation to be fully awake to the cyclones swirling around them. They accept that the old "safe" world is gone. Their anxiety is the vibration of an engine running at a speed the old corporate structures weren't built to handle.

The younger generation isn't breaking the rules.
Most of them don't even know the old rules exist.

Whether I am in Silicon Valley, Dubai, Korea, or Norway, I can spot future-ready people immediately. By their approach. They see possibility in chaos. They need purpose, not certainty. They use the current's energy to move faster while others exhaust themselves fighting it.

What they are using, consciously or instinctively, is a navigation approach built for Emergence. Five elements that work together. P.E.A.C.E., which will be covered in detail in Chapters 4–8, stops the war against reality.

What Future-Ready Navigators Do Differently

Watch how future-ready people move and patterns emerge. Consistent approaches that work in Emergence.

- **Navigate by energy.** If something drains energy, stop. Intuitive recognition that exhaustion is expensive. The body processes information faster than conscious thought. Body-based navigation is future-ready leadership. They spot the room where people nod but don't commit. They catch the hesitation before someone agrees to an impossible deadline. They register the project that checks every box but sits wrong in the gut. Projects that energize get resources.

Your gut is not "soft."

It's processing what your head can't keep up with.

- **Build networks.** Recognition flows to whoever solves the problem, regardless of title. Collaboration happens through channels leadership doesn't know exist. Expertise gets shared through sandbox sessions that bypass training departments.

- **Treat AI like electricity, infrastructure.** While committees form to study GenAI tools, navigators are using Copilot and Claude to automate workflows, generate content, analyze patterns. Learning by doing, failing fast, adjusting faster. AI isn't replacing humans but amplifying those who act.[1]
- **Create evidence.** Accumulate demonstrations. The portfolio matters more than the résumé. The GitHub repository outweighs the Grade Point Average (GPA). Deliver, then improve.
- **Test constantly.** Every idea is an experiment. Every project is a prototype. Every decision is reversible until it's not. Fail fast at ten things rather than succeed slowly at one. In emergence, speed of learning beats depth of planning.
- **Respond deliberately.** Reaction is biological, immediate, fear-driven. Response is intentional and purpose-aligned. Fast decisions that aren't rushed. Quick pivots that aren't random. The Speed Cyclone demands velocity, not panic.
- **Integrate everything.** Work-life balance assumes separation. The side project becomes the main gig. The network becomes the net worth. Emergence doesn't respect compartments.
- **And they've redefined risk entirely.** The biggest risk isn't moving too fast. It's staying still while everything moves.

These aren't rules to follow. These are patterns that emerge when people stop fighting reality and start working with it.

Seeing Natural Navigators Clearly

The misunderstandings run deep. Leaders trained in traditional management see problems where there's actually evolution.

- **"Lazy."** The person who leaves at 3 p.m. to coach soccer manages energy, not hours. The one who ignores weekend emails protects capacity for what matters. Energy is finite and impact is what counts. Future-ready people work intensely on what matters and give nothing to what doesn't.

- **"Entitled."** Expecting flexibility when technology enables it is practical, not entitled. Demanding purpose-aligned work recognizes that abundance without meaning is poverty. The old employment contract is dead. Seeing this clearly is awareness, not entitlement.
- **"Disloyal."** Look where loyalty actually flows. To leaders who share equity generously. To teams that deliver on promises. To companies actually living their stated purpose. Natural navigators show fierce loyalty, just not to empty structures.
- **"Impatient."** Executives implementing AI while peers debate its risks. Builders shipping solutions while committees schedule meetings about meetings. Recent graduates delivering products while others perfect proposals. This is emergence speed. Reality doesn't wait for approval processes.
- **"Need training."** The designer who taught herself 3D modeling through online tutorials. The executive who learned coding with AI from Reddit threads. The analyst who mastered data visualization from YouTube. Self-taught using resources traditional education ignores. These people need opportunity and resources, not remedial instruction.
- **"Don't understand business."** They understand that the whole concept of business is transforming. That shareholder value without stakeholder value is unsustainable. That profit without purpose is hollow. They see the evolution of business with clear eyes.
- **"Can't handle pressure."** Pressure is fine. Chronic biological alarm for no purpose is not. There is a difference between meaningful intensity and manufactured urgency, between necessary sprints and permanent emergency mode. Future-ready people preserve biological resources for what matters.

These patterns appear everywhere, in every generation, in people who have stopped fighting emergence and started navigating it. Leaders trying to correct these behaviors are attempting to fix exactly what makes navigators valuable.

When Organizations Learn from the Next Generation

Cisco's leaders invested heavily in college recruitment by targeting the brightest minds with the latest capabilities, running extensive graduate programs across engineering, sales, and multiple divisions. They spent substantial money getting talented young people on board, training them, preparing them for corporate success.

Then, as soon as the "golden handcuffs" came off, they quit.

Turnover was massive. The pattern repeated across divisions. Cisco's leaders believed they knew the problem: these young people didn't know how to work in a corporate environment. Traditional education hadn't prepared them to be employable, it prepared them to know things, but not how to interact in the corporate world. After losing millions, the Business Unit leader reached out to my company, Next Step.

The initial request to our team: "Teach them how to work in a corporate environment."

Unlike most consulting firms that diagnose problems, advise on solutions, or deliver training, we work differently—using the P.E.A.C.E. process to deliver lasting results.

When I asked what the senior leader really wanted to achieve, he responded: "Integrate young talent into the organization." With this clarity we moved into exploration. What's actually causing them to leave?

The answer was not what Cisco's leaders assumed. It wasn't a lack of knowledge or skills, it was their experience of the workplace.

The college graduates came with new ideas, fresh perspectives, different ways of operating. They brought their own culture. And Cisco, like many organizations, was trying to put them in boxes that didn't fit.

The solution wasn't training young people to adapt to Cisco. It was empowering four generations to work together, collaborating to explore new approaches, learn from one another, and co-create a future-ready culture that works for all.

We equipped the managers with tools to coach, support, champion, and learn from these bright, demanding young people. We enabled the younger generation to work with, not fight against, their leaders.

The measurable change: turnover reduced significantly. Productivity and revenue increased by more than 200 percent as Cisco adopted new future-ready leadership approaches instead of forcing everyone into old patterns.

**Those who question the system aren't the problem.
The boxes are.**

This work wasn't unique to Cisco. Since then, we have delivered solutions for multiple organizations facing the same multigenerational workforce challenge. The pattern is consistent: organizations spending millions recruiting the next generation, then losing them by demanding they abandon what makes them valuable.

> **Why Are Your Best Young Hires Walking Out the Door?**
>
> Wilson Sonsini Goodrich & Rosati, a prominent legal firm based in Silicon Valley which represents giants from Apple to Google, was rapidly losing hope. Young attorneys with exceptional credentials, recruited from top law schools as junior attorneys, resigned within one year. The legal industry's traditional partnership track didn't align with how the next generation viewed careers, contribution, or success.
>
> The answer was the same: stop trying to force emerging talent into established boxes. Create space for managers and young professionals to learn from each other. Empower both to shape how the work gets done. The result was similar: reduced turnover, increased innovation, retained talent that competitors kept losing.

The work we have done with Cisco, Wilson Sonsini, Eli Lilly, and numerous other organizations demonstrates that the challenge isn't the people. It's systems designed for a world that no longer exists.

When Transformation Isn't Optional: Adobe's Navigation

When the 2008 financial crisis hit, most companies went defensive. Cut costs, delay innovation, ride it out. Leaders in Adobe did the opposite. They committed to dismantling the business model that had made them billions and replacing it with something that didn't exist yet.

Our team led that transformation from the inside. Forty people from Next Step working collaboratively with Adobe's teams for years. Not consultants delivering reports. Partners in the war rooms, day and night, figuring it out together.

> *The Adobe story runs as a thread through this book because it's the clearest example of every element of the P.E.A.C.E. methodology in action. One sentence from a CEO became the most powerful act of empowerment I've ever witnessed. Tiger teams tested ideas with actual customers in days, not months. The angriest critics became co-creators. And a company that started by moving software to the cloud ended up reshaping an industry. See Chapter 10 for the full story of how Adobe's transformation touched all aspects of P.E.A.C.E.*

The Bridge Navigators Are Building

Navigators aren't destroying anything. They're building bridges to what's next, often while others are still defending what was.

They're redefining professionalism. The person analyzing code in a hoodie is more professional than the one perfecting PowerPoints in a tie.

They're creating new structures on the fly. Networks that form around problems and dissolve when they're solved. Authority that flows to competence. Structures that breathe rather than calcify. These structures work because they match emergence: fluid, responsive, purpose-driven.

The transformation is internal before it's external. Mindset before method. You can't navigate emergence with Industrial Age thinking any more than you can drive a car with horse-riding skills. The navigators understand this: transformation starts between your ears, not in your org chart.

Most importantly, they're not random in their navigation. There's a pattern, a system, an approach that works whether someone is 22 or 62. Whether they're in Silicon Valley or Stuttgart. Whether they're building a startup or transforming a corporation.

This navigation system has five elements that work together. You already know its name. Part II shows how it works.

Your Turn: Future-Ready Navigators' Reflection

Are you fighting Emergence or flowing with it?

About the navigators around you:

- Who in your organization moves with flow instead of exhaustion?
- What would the youngest person on your team do with your authority?
- Who's building something while others are still planning?
- Which "problem employee" will actually be your best navigator?

About the misunderstandings:

- Which behaviors in employees are you trying to "fix" that will actually be adaptations?
- Where is "laziness" actually selective energy management?
- What looks like disloyalty that's really just evolution?
- Which "lack of respect" is actually respect for competence over position?

About your own navigation:

- Where are you still fighting reality that won't change?
- What would you do differently if stability never returned?
- Which exhausting processes exist only because they always have?
- Where will less control create more value?

About future-readiness:

- Are you willing to learn from someone younger?
- Can you release expertise that no longer serves?
- Would you follow someone without a title who has competence?
- What if the problem isn't them but the system they're revealing?

The answers matter less than the recognition: emergence rewards navigators, not controllers. And navigation can be learned.

These navigators, whether 22 or 62, share one quality above all: curiosity over certainty. They'd rather explore what they don't know than defend what they do.

The exhaustion people feel isn't from working harder. It's from the constant biological cost of fighting what can't be controlled.

Fear isn't going anywhere. But it doesn't have to be in charge.

P.E.A.C.E. is about ending the war with reality. And that begins with Purpose, the North Star that guides when all other navigation fails.

PART II

Navigating with P.E.A.C.E.

> "You cannot buy the revolution.
> You cannot make the revolution.
> You can only be the revolution.
> It is in your spirit, or it is nowhere."
>
> —Ursula K. Le Guin, *The Dispossessed* (2024 [1974])

In 1999, a 19-year-old college dropout named Shawn Fanning released Napster and accidentally destroyed the music industry's business model. Not through strategic planning or market analysis. Through curiosity about sharing songs with friends.

The recording industry responded exactly as Industrial Age thinking demanded: lawsuits, lobbying, control. They spent hundreds of millions fighting reality while future-ready navigators simply moved to new platforms. The industry that had controlled music distribution for a century exhausted itself fighting reality it couldn't change.

Meanwhile, a computer company in Cupertino watched the chaos and asked a different question. Not "How do we stop this?" but "What does this make possible?"

Steve Jobs didn't fight the emergence of digital music. He navigated it.[1] iTunes launched in 2001, the iPod changed everything, and Apple, a computer company, became the world's largest music retailer. Not by predicting the future but by reading the patterns everyone else was fighting.

The difference wasn't resources. The recording industry had more money, more lawyers, more power. The difference was navigation. While they exhausted themselves trying to control, Apple focused on creating. While they defended territory, Apple worked with the way the world was going.

This pattern appears everywhere. Those who fight emergence exhaust themselves. Those who navigate it thrive.

The Industrial Age created unprecedented wealth and prosperity through structure: clear roles, measurable output, career paths that rewarded loyalty. That approach worked for more than a century and built the foundation everything stands on today. But the conditions that made those structures effective have shifted. And the people who built their success on them face the hardest question: what do you keep and what do you let go?

Meanwhile, future-ready navigators build the future around them. Some leaders add complexity to manage chaos while others find simplicity through purpose. Some experts defend expertise while beginners solve problems differently.

Think of honeybees. When their hive gets too warm, they do not panic or hold emergency meetings. They simply move to the entrance and fan their wings. Each bee responding to local conditions, no central coordination needed, perfect collective result. Emergence in action.

Future-ready leaders navigate using different principles. Five elements that work together: Purpose, Exploration, Action, Collaboration, Empowerment. P.E.A.C.E.

This is the navigation needed for today's inflection point. Success emerges through use, not through study.

Traditional change management assumes change is an event to deal with between stable states. Plan the change, implement the change, sustain the change. But emergence isn't change, it's continuous evolution. You can't manage it. You can only navigate through it.

Industrial Age leadership development focused on competencies to master. Strategic thinking, decision-making, communication. But emergence doesn't respect competencies. It rewards capabilities that emerge through practice, not skills that get certified.

Traditional frameworks promise control through complexity. More process, more structure, more oversight. But complexity doesn't lead to control in emergence. It creates friction that slows navigation exactly when speed matters most.

P.E.A.C.E. works because it matches Emergence reality. Fluid not fixed. Purpose-driven, not plan-dependent. It creates stability through movement—like riding a bicycle, stop moving and you fall over.

The future-ready navigators in Part I, whether age 22 or 62, are not using different tools. They are using tools differently.

Leaders in the recording industry had every advantage except one: they could not stop fighting reality that had already changed. Future-ready leaders learn from that mistake.

The navigation system is learnable. The question isn't whether you'll need it. You already do. The question is whether you'll build it before the next cyclone hits.

Each chapter in this part covers one letter of the P.E.A.C.E. methodology:

- **Chapter 4, Purpose,** builds the internal compass that makes every decision possible—even when external direction has disappeared. You will see how Fortune 100 leaders anchored their organizations to purpose when markets, structures, and strategies were shifting beneath them.
- **Chapter 5, Exploration,** teaches you to move into the unknown without losing your footing—a discipline called bounded discovery. This is not about experimentation for its own sake. It is about developing the capacity to learn faster than conditions change.

- **Chapter 6, Action,** breaks the paralysis loop. Most leaders know what needs to happen. What stops them is the absence of confidence. This chapter shows exactly how—and when—to move anyway.
- **Chapter 7, Collaboration,** demonstrates that shared purpose is not a soft concept. It is a force multiplier. The leaders and organizations navigating emergence most effectively are doing it together—and this chapter shows you how to build that kind of momentum.
- **Chapter 8, Empowerment,** is the chapter most organizations miss—and the one most responsible for whether transformation lasts. This chapter shows you how to release what your people are already capable of and build an organization that can move without you leading every step.

But it all starts in the same place. Purpose. The North Star that doesn't move—even when everything around you is in motion.

4 Purpose: Your Destination Through Emergence

"Don't ask what the world needs.

Ask what makes you come alive, and go do it.

Because what the world needs is people who have come alive."

—Howard Thurman, theologian and civil rights leader

In 1996, Marvel Entertainment filed for bankruptcy. The company that created the big-screen versions of Spider-Man, the X-Men, and the Avengers was buried under $610 million in debt and falling. After emerging from bankruptcy under new ownership, they were still desperate for cash. So they started selling their characters. Spider-Man went to Sony for $7 million. The X-Men went to Fox. The Fantastic Four followed. Each deal brought cash but fractured the universe Stan Lee and Jack Kirby had built over decades.[1]

The smart money said keep selling. Wall Street valued Marvel's parts more than its whole. The board saw licensing deals as survival. Every

MBA-trained analysis reached the same conclusion: maximize asset value through individual character monetization.

But Kevin Feige saw something different. Feige had started as an assistant to producer Lauren Shuler Donner and worked his way up through Marvel's film projects. When he became president of production at Marvel Studios in 2007, he understood something the spreadsheets missed. Marvel was not a portfolio of characters to monetize. It was a universe of interconnected stories. The purpose was not maximum extraction from individual properties. It was creating modern mythology that mattered to millions.[2]

Feige and the Marvel Studios' leadership made a decision that Wall Street called insane. Instead of selling more characters, Marvel would risk everything to maintain creative control. They put their remaining characters up as collateral for a $525 million loan, bet on building their own cinematic universe, and cast Robert Downey Jr., an actor who studios would not insure, as Iron Man. They would connect every film to create something that had never existed: a shared narrative universe spanning decades.[3]

Marvel held to its North Star: creating a universe of meaning through modern mythology. Every decision filtered through that purpose. Which characters to introduce when. Which stories served the larger narrative and which risks were worth taking.

By 2019, the Marvel Cinematic Universe had generated more than $22 billion in box office revenue, becoming the highest-grossing film franchise of all time. Disney bought Marvel Entertainment for $4 billion in 2009. A company that had been worth less than nothing during bankruptcy, buried under $610 million in debt, sold for $4 billion just over a decade later.[4]

Better purpose, not better spreadsheets. They saw characters as stories that connect humans, not assets to extract. They built long-term value instead of maximizing short-term licensing revenue. Purpose as navigation, not marketing.

Adobe's transformation shows a similar trajectory. Purpose-driven transformation that Wall Street initially punished but that reshaped an entire industry.[5,6]

But Marvel's organizational purpose only worked because it aligned with thousands of individual purposes. Kevin Feige's personal mission to create modern mythology. Every writer who believed that stories shape culture. Every designer who saw these characters as more than entertainment.

The same was true for Adobe. Before Shantanu Narayen could transform the company's business model, he had to step away from the external noise. Only then could Adobe's true purpose to "Enable Creativity for All" emerge.

But here's what most people miss about Adobe's story. Narayen didn't find the purpose in a boardroom. It came from getting clear on his own purpose first—to carry forward and expand what Adobe's founders started.

Organizational purpose without personal purpose is just words on walls. Personal purpose must come first. Without it, you get WeWork claiming to "elevate consciousness" while the CEO cashes out. You get companies with beautiful mission statements and exhausted employees who can't explain why their work matters.

Real purpose, the kind that transforms companies and industries, is born inside individuals.

Purpose is not a poster on the wall.
It's the filter that tells you what to stop doing today.

Finding Your Purpose

People don't "get purpose" from an expert, book, or weekend retreat. They don't acquire it like a commodity. Purpose exists within, waiting to emerge once inherited expectations get cleared away.

When each person comes into this world, there's a reason. Each of us is here for a purpose, the impact our soul came to make.

Children often have clear sense of purpose and direction. Full of creativity and curiosity, asking "what if?" But boxes start blocking them: go to school, get a job, make money, achieve status. Each box adds clutter until purpose gets obscured by Industrial Age conditioning.

If someone is unsure of their purpose, it's not lost. It's buried.

Purpose isn't what you do.
It's why you can't stop doing it.

Uncovering purpose requires going inside. Step out of the box. Create space without activity, requirements, or expectations. Nature works for many people. Silence works for others.

Look at what energizes you. What are you proudest of? Not the achievement that impressed others, but the one that made you feel really good inside. A product built, a difference made, a moment when work didn't feel like work.

Purpose isn't a one-time calendar activity. It's a daily practice—listening to your inner voice. Thirty minutes for a nature walk, meditation, or quietly asking "what do I really want to achieve?" The method matters less than the consistency.

Over time this works because purpose is already there inside you. Identifying it requires clearing away what's blocking the view.

Recognizing Real Versus False Purpose

How does someone know when they've found their actual purpose versus what they think they should want?

Real purpose feels different from manufactured goals. When people discover their true North Star, several things happen.

The body knows first. There's a physical sensation, energy rather than exhaustion when thinking about it. The body leans forward.

Clarity replaces confusion. Suddenly, past experiences form a pattern. That random job, that "failed" project, that unexpected passion, they were all navigation toward this North Star.

Fear transforms into urgency. The risk of staying still becomes more terrifying than the risk of moving forward.

External validation becomes irrelevant. When purpose emerges from within, the need for approval disappears. Parents' expectations, society's definitions of success, peer comparisons all lose their grip. The internal compass overrides external noise.

Decisions become obvious. When Adobe CEO Narayen saw Adobe's true purpose, abandoning the profitable licensing model was the only decision. Purpose acts like a filter, making choices clear even when they're hard.

Marie's purpose fit into five words: keep people safe and warm. At 19, that meant standing at a bridge talking soldiers into surrender. At 85, after her daughter died, it meant knitting hats for strangers. The circumstances changed completely. The purpose never did. If your purpose needs a paragraph to explain, it's probably not purpose. It's positioning.

I don't care if your purpose sounds impressive in board meetings unless it changes what you do on Monday morning.

Real purpose doesn't need motivation. It ***is*** motivation.

When Personal Purpose Becomes Clear

Suresh left everything behind in Mumbai to work 80-hour weeks in Silicon Valley, sharing a small apartment with three other engineers. No family. No social life. No work-life balance concerns.

Why?

His North Star: develop technology to prevent cancer deaths. He watched his mother die from lung cancer that could have been prevented with better early detection tools. That's his purpose. His reason for being on this planet.

Emergence means no separation between work and purpose. When work ***is*** integral to achieving one's North Star, "work-life balance" becomes irrelevant.

When Suresh interviewed for jobs, he wasn't seeking comfort or foosball tables. He didn't need career development workshops. He showed up with absolute confidence born from internal clarity.

Anchored from Within

Internal purpose generates self-reliance that external validation could never provide. When personal purpose aligns with work, engagement is natural. An 80-hour week isn't exhausting, it's fulfillment.

At 17, Sarah from Congo stood before 95 international peers at Oxford with stunning clarity: "My purpose is to solve hunger problems in my village through finding ways in our arid environment to develop fruit."

Not "I want to help people." Not "I'm interested in agriculture." A specific achievement she intends to accomplish in her lifetime.

Sarah's comments were shared during my keynote for the Oxford Summer Program and spoken with more clarity than most CEOs I've worked with. She's not future-ready because she read the right books.

She's future-ready because hunger and lived experience gave her a purpose no amount of Industrial Age conditioning could bury.

My own purpose didn't arrive fully formed. At 17, it was simple: get out, pay rent, survive. At 18: get a business degree. In my twenties: "don't be homeless, prove I'm something better than I had been told I was." My purpose was specific and tangible at every stage. It evolved as I did.

That's the point. Purpose isn't something you discover once at a retreat and carry forever unchanged. It emerges through experience. Each stage of my life sharpened it. Survival became stability. Stability became empowerment. Empowerment became global impact. The thread was always there, but I could only see it looking back.

Suresh, Sarah, and I demonstrate the same principle: when individual purpose becomes clear internally, career decisions become obvious. Suresh works with Novartis because their oncology mission serves his North Star. Sarah pursues agri-tech internships advancing her village transformation goals.

They're not optimizing for job security or prestigious careers. They're optimizing for purpose alignment that delivers engagement that can't be bought or managed.

This resonates powerfully with younger professionals, who watched their parents sacrifice purpose for security and still lose both in economic downturns. They enter the workforce already knowing that traditional job security is a myth. They'd rather align with purpose from day one than chase illusions of stability.

The "Not Nice" Truth About Purpose

Years ago, colleague Bill Jamaica looked me straight in the eye: "You are not a nice person."

Most people would be devastated. I was curious.

He continued: "You're a fucking kick-ass, get-shit-done, efficient, effective, successful person. There's no room for nice in that."

He was right. That was one of the most valuable insights anyone ever gave me as it confirmed I was navigating toward my purpose—making a difference through real business results.

Nice is the enemy of purpose.

When someone is truly purpose-driven, when they are clearly focused on their North Star and use courage to pursue it regardless of what others think, they don't have the luxury of being nice. They are committed to being effective.

Nice people don't tell high performers their work isn't meeting standards. Nice people don't make hard personnel decisions when someone's actions don't align with objectives.

Purpose-driven people build the future.

I don't care if people think my feedback is harsh. I don't care if they describe my process as "challenging" because I expect them to achieve what they committed to.

I care about impact. I care about building something that changes the world.

When the choice is between making people comfortable and making progress toward the North Star, future-ready leaders choose progress. Every time. Without apology.

Prioritize effectiveness over comfort, truth over pleasantries.

Younger professionals get this instinctively. They've grown up watching "nice" companies make "nice" statements while destroying the planet and exploiting workers. They prefer brutal honesty to comfortable lies. They'd rather work for someone who's clear about expectations than someone who's nice while the company fails.

Purpose without sustainability is short-term thinking. There are no profits on a dead planet. Future-ready companies integrate environmental and social sustainability into purpose, not as nice-to-have but as survival requirement. The next generation won't work for, buy from, or invest in companies destroying what they'll inherit.

This is standard in Silicon Valley. Steve Goodman, CEO of SonicWall, demonstrated it perfectly. I was driving to their office in San Francisco to prepare for a critical client meeting. I arrived late, clearly flustered only 15 minutes before the client. I had been in an accident on the freeway, my car was damaged, and my head was spinning. When Steve asked "How are you?" I instinctively launched into the story of the accident.

He looked at his watch. Fifteen minutes until the client arrived. He said: "Sounds like a personal issue. Now how do you suggest we approach the contract issue with the client during the meeting?"

Not cruel. Not uncaring. Focused. We had 15 minutes to prepare for something that mattered to the business. My car situation, real as it was, didn't advance that purpose. Steve wasn't being mean, he could see I was OK. He was being effective. That's Silicon Valley leadership: focus on what moves the business forward, not what makes people comfortable.

SonicWall scaled. Became profitable. Was acquired successfully. Because leaders like Steve didn't confuse niceness with kindness or comfort with care. They cared enough about the business and the people depending on it to stay focused on what actually mattered.

When individuals achieve this clarity, this not-nice, uncompromising personal purpose, organizational transformation becomes possible. Not the other way around.

The Most Important 30 Seconds of an Interview

Often I am asked to interview final candidates for key roles within clients' organizations. Every interview starts the same way. Before discussing experience, capabilities, or expectations, I ask one question: "What do you believe is your primary purpose in life?"

The answer determines everything.

Let's say the company's purpose is to create a more sustainable ocean and Earth through innovative logistics. The candidate responds: "I really want to contribute to well-being in society and organizations."

For me the interview is over. I ask a few more polite questions while thinking "It's been lovely to meet you. Have a good life." After 20 minutes I thank them and close the meeting.

That person will never thrive in an organization focused on ocean sustainability. They'll become disengaged, regardless of salary or perks. They'll be working against their internal compass every single day.

But when another candidate says, "I believe my purpose is to make a difference to the planet, especially the health of our oceans," now there's a conversation. Even if they lack certain capabilities, even if they're junior, we can explore how their current capabilities will advance both their purpose and ours. The alignment doesn't have to be perfect.

Maybe someone's purpose is improving ocean health but they're currently working in healthcare AI. The performance review discussion becomes: "What do you love about your current role?" "I love working with AI. I'm already thinking about how what I'm learning now could eventually apply to ocean sustainability." "Great, let's have you take on more AI-related logistics projects as this is a critical requirement in healthcare for humans as well as in marine sustainability."

Most recruitment fails because people in organizations hire for skills and hope for purpose alignment. But skills without shared purpose create disengaged employees counting days until something better appears.

When purposes align, everything else becomes solvable. When they don't, no amount of money or benefits will create engagement.

Thirty seconds in an interview saves everyone years of frustration. Both parties deserve work that feeds their purpose, not fights it.

Constancy When Everything Shifts

Purpose isn't a mission statement on your lobby wall or the word-smithed paragraph consultants charged six figures to write. It's not the aspirational vision that changes with every new CEO.

Purpose is the North Star that guides when everything else moves. Markets shift, technology transforms, teams change, purpose remains. Sailors navigated by the North Star for millennia because it stays fixed while everything else moves. In emergence, you need that fixed point more than ever.

What Purpose Actually Is (and Isn't)

Real purpose has specific qualities:

- **Purpose is identity, not strategy.** Strategy is what you do. Purpose is who you are. When Adobe shifted from selling software licenses to subscriptions, strategy changed completely. But purpose remained: empowering creativity. During that crisis, CEO Shantanu Narayen asked: "What are we actually here to do?" The answer wasn't in market analysis. It was felt in the bones of everyone who joined Adobe because creativity mattered.

  Steve Jobs's purpose was changing how people live through technology. When Apple launched the iPhone, he didn't rest. He continued working until his dying moment, navigating by that same North Star.

- **Purpose is felt before it's articulated.** You know it in your gut before your head finds words. Marvel's purpose lived in everyone who understood these weren't just characters but modern myths. When purpose is real, people feel it without explanation. When it's manufactured, people perform it while secretly wondering what they're doing.
- **Purpose costs something.** If your purpose doesn't require sacrifice, it's not purpose but preference. Marvel risked bankruptcy to maintain their universe rather than maximize licensing. Adobe cancelled agreements with partners that didn't align with cloud transformation. Patagonia tells customers not to buy jackets they don't need, literally running Black Friday ads saying "Don't Buy This Jacket" because overconsumption violates their purpose.
- **Purpose survives contact with reality.** Markets transform overnight, technology makes industries obsolete but purpose remains constant. The tools changed. The purpose didn't. Purpose adapts tactics while maintaining truth.
- **Purpose creates energy rather than consuming it.** False purpose exhausts everyone. Real purpose energizes. It turns work from extraction into contribution. The energy emerges from meaning, not motivation.

When 70 percent of younger professionals say they'd take a pay cut for purpose alignment, they're being practical, not idealistic. They watched their parents burn out chasing metrics that didn't matter. They understand purpose alignment determines whether work becomes fulfilling or soul-crushing.

Purpose is about clarity. Clear enough that decisions make themselves, that people self-select in or out, that when Emergence (or emergence of new requirements) accelerates there is something real to offer.

When Organizations Navigate by Purpose

Shortly before the pandemic, my firm was engaged by the Ticketmaster board as they merged with Live Nation. There was a critical problem: Ticketmaster had become synonymous with frustrating transactions.

Customers hated the fees, the process, the experience. Competitors offered ticket sales with less hassle and lower costs. Event producers had alternatives.

The company held the number one position in event ticketing, but that position was eroding. They needed transformation, not optimization.

The shift started at the board level with the fundamental question: what are you really trying to achieve? The answer wasn't "sell more tickets" or "block the competitors." It was deeper: how do we differentiate ourselves and move out of a transactional, low-margin, highly competitive environment into something genuinely value-added?

That purpose clarity opened exploration. What do people actually want when they attend events? What are others doing in experience creation? What does "buying an event" mean beyond the ticket itself?

The exploration revealed the shift: people didn't just want access to events. They wanted to build and share their experience. The videos, the selfies, the VIP moments, the social proof that they were there. The ticket was the beginning, not the end.

Action meant restructuring the entire go-to-market approach. Not "go to Ticketmaster to buy a ticket" but "go to Ticketmaster to begin your event experience." Integrate video capture, social sharing, VIP access, everything that makes attending memorable. Stay with Ticketmaster for the experience. Buy just a ticket elsewhere if that's all you need.

The messaging and market positioning shifted completely, from ticket sales to event experiences.

This was pre-pandemic timing, perfect for a company that needed to differentiate before the world forced everyone to rethink live events entirely. The shift from transactional to experiential wasn't just strategy; it was survival disguised as innovation.

Our strategic work with Genentech reinforced this pattern. When biotech companies navigate breakthrough science versus commercial viability, purpose clarity becomes survival. How do you maintain groundbreaking research while creating sustainable growth?

Defining objectives, key results (OKRs) and incentives always starts with: what are you actually trying to achieve with this initiative? Not "be profitable" or "discover new drugs," but the deeper purpose that guides decisions and drives commitment.

Scaling with Purpose

Sugar Bowl Bakery faced the same question when growth threatened what made them special. A family-led West Coast baking company known for quality and natural ingredients had opportunities for mass distribution. Most family businesses at this crossroads choose: stay small and maintain values, or scale and compromise quality.

I worked with them to ask: what's the actual purpose? Not "be a bakery" but specifically what impact do we want to have on the world?

Growth while retaining quality. Natural ingredients. People inclusion through every level of expansion. Those weren't nice-to-haves. They were non-negotiables that shaped every decision about scaling.

Sugar Bowl Bakery is now a globally recognized provider of high-quality pastries through mass distribution because they refused to abandon their principles. Purpose focused growth on what mattered.

The Constellation of Purpose: When Purpose Aligns Across Levels

In truly future-ready companies, purpose isn't hanging on a sign by the elevator. People live it. Breathe it. Fight through obstacles to reach this North Star every single day.

Think about what a constellation actually is. Individual stars—each burning with its own energy, its own position, its own intensity. Alone, they're just scattered points of light. But step back, and those same stars form something larger. A recognizable pattern. A navigation tool that has guided humanity for thousands of years.

Success happens when individual purpose aligns with organizational purpose. Each person has their own North Star. The organization creates the pattern that connects those individual purposes into something greater. Future-ready managers set departmental goals aligned with the organizational North Star.

Remember Suresh? His personal fire and Novartis's oncology mission point the same way. His manager Jane recruited him for oncology research to align his cancer-fighting purpose with business objectives.

When projects addressing treatment of lung cancer emerge, Suresh gets first consideration. Not for his résumé. For purpose alignment. That creates energy no bonus structure could ever manufacture.

Figure 4.1 shows the power of alignment across the organization. By assigning Suresh to the oncology team, he advances toward his own purpose of reducing lung cancer while accelerating progress toward Novartis's North Star—enhancing people's lives.

When individual purposes connect to team purpose, and team purpose connects to the organization's purpose, the result is energy that can't be manufactured through motivational programs. You'll see this pattern multiply further in Chapter 7 when we look at how cross-functional collaboration succeeds precisely because people's individual purposes align with the same destination, even when they navigate from different positions.

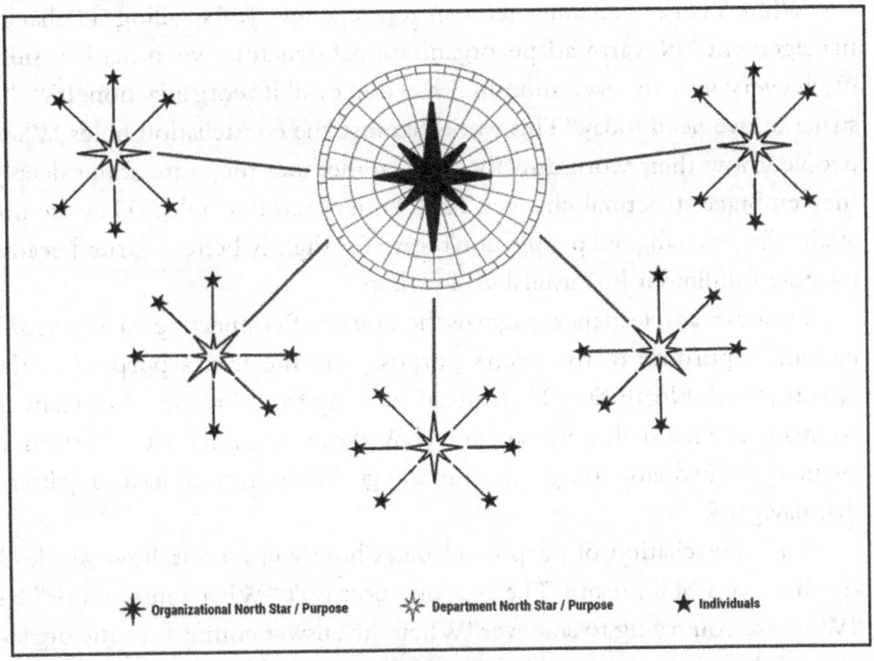

Figure 4.1 Constellation of purpose.

When purpose don't align, you get the opposite. Talented people doing competent work without energy behind it. Checking boxes. Counting days. Performing engagement while quietly searching for something that actually matters to them. No amount of salary, benefits, or office perks fixes purpose misalignment. It's structural, not motivational.

Adobe discovered this during their cloud transformation. The organizational purpose remained clear: empowering creativity. But each engineer, each designer, each salesperson had to find their own connection to that purpose in a completely new context. Some found it in reaching creators who could never afford a $2,500 software license. Others found it in enabling collaboration in a way that could not have happened using desktop tools.

Some employees couldn't find it and left. That's not failure. That's the constellation working exactly as it should. People whose purpose aligns stay and contribute more. People whose purpose doesn't align move toward something that serves their own North Star better.

While many companies reorganize every few years calling it "change management," Novartis adapts organizational structure when markets shift, often every four to seven months. They don't call it reorganization. It's "the structure we need today." This works because the constellation holds. When people know their work directly serves something they care about deeply, they embrace structural changes. They understand the "why." They are not afraid. Purpose-aligned people don't leave for slightly better salaries because purpose fulfillment isn't available elsewhere.

Future-ready leaders recognize the power of connecting each person's individual purpose to the team's purpose, and the team's purpose to the organization's North Star. That thread running from individual to team to company is what makes alignment real. Without it, you have a collection of talented individuals doing separate things. With it, you have a pattern that navigates.

The constellation of purpose changes how you recruit, how you lead, and how you build teams. The first question isn't "What can you do?" It's "What are you trying to achieve?" When the answer connects to the organization's North Star, everything else becomes solvable. Capabilities can be developed. Experience can be gained. But purpose alignment either exists or it doesn't.

In Chapter 8, you'll see how empowerment becomes a force that doesn't need managing when the constellation is in place. People who are purpose-aligned and given authority don't need supervision. They need boundaries and trust.

The Courage to Cut What's Working

Leading with purpose is brutal. Not peaceful. Not comfortable. Not safe. Purpose creates tension that never fully resolves. These paradoxes aren't problems to solve. They're dynamics to navigate.

Purpose Creates Tension You Can't Resolve

This is the fear test. The one question that cuts through anxiety faster than any other: **what's the worst that can happen? And how will it impact achievement of your purpose?**

Get specific. How does this worst-case scenario affect your North Star?

Most fears collapse under this test. You lose the client. Does that prevent you from having lasting impact on people and business? No. The company rejects your idea. Does that block all paths to your North Star? It almost never does.

The fears that survive deserve attention. They're usually showing you something real about misalignment, not risk. If the worst case genuinely threatens your purpose, you're either on the wrong path or you haven't found the right approach yet.

Purpose-driven decisions feel risky. They usually aren't. Even in worst-case scenarios, your purpose remains. The path changes. The timeline stretches. The destination stays clear.

Saying No More Than Yes

For every opportunity that aligns, ten won't. For every partnership that fits, twenty don't. The North Star isn't just about where you're going. It's about what you're willing to abandon to get there.

During Adobe's transformation, leaders had to say no to customers demanding perpetual licenses. No to dealers who'd built businesses on boxed software. No to employees whose expertise was suddenly obsolete.

Each "no" cost relationships, revenue, reputation. Saying yes to those requests would have cost purpose. The conflict didn't weaken Adobe's direction. It sharpened it.

Most leaders fail at purpose because they cannot defend it. They add "and also" until purpose becomes everything, which means it's nothing. "We empower creativity *and* maximize shareholder value *and* serve communities *and* lead innovation *and* ..." That's a wish list, not a purpose.

When Purpose Has a Cost

In December 2017, Yvon Chouinard sued the Trump administration for slashing Bears Ears National Monument in Utah by 85 percent. He joined a coalition of conservation groups and Native American tribes to challenge the largest elimination of protected land in American history. People inside the company worried about mixing business with politics. Some questioned whether the move would alienate conservative customers.

Chouinard's response was his company's mission: "We're in business to save our home planet." If that clarity costs customers who don't share the purpose, the loss is really a win.

I tell clients: "If your focus on purpose doesn't offend someone, you need to rethink your actions." Not offensive in trying to harm. Offensive in taking a stand. In choosing. In saying "this" matters more than "that."

The clearer your purpose, the more people it excludes. That terrifies leaders trained to maximize market share and capture everyone. But the Meaning Cyclone rewards depth over breadth. Resonance over reach. Trying to matter to everyone means mattering to no one. Your purpose should make some people say "that's not for me."

Purpose is personal before it is organizational. Purpose cannot be assigned. Meaning cannot be mandated. I discovered this when everything felt like it was collapsing. In chaos, my purpose clarified: "Empower people to succeed." That purpose doesn't need a corner office or money. It remains the core of every decision I make, professionally and personally.

Every organizational purpose is carried by individual purposes. If people can't connect their personal purpose to the organizational one, you have compliance, not alignment.

Purpose clarifies which options matter.

Letting Go of Activity Addiction

Purpose requires the discipline of saying no. Constantly. To tasks that seem urgent but aren't important. To initiatives that would make you look busy but not effective. To the "can you do this?" requests that fill calendars while emptying impact.

This connects directly to being "not nice." Nice people say yes when asked. Effective people ask "does this advance our North Star?" before answering. Nice people worry about disappointing others. Purpose-driven people worry about disappointing themselves by spending time on what doesn't matter.

Letting go of expectations means letting go of should: "We should probably be in that meeting." "We should explore that opportunity." "We should respond to that request." Should is the enemy of focused. When everything feels like something you should do, nothing gets done that actually moves purpose forward.

Disney's CEO Bob Iger nailed prioritization: "If I have more than three priorities, I don't have any priorities."[7] Most leaders have twenty. Which means they have zero. Future-ready leaders ruthlessly focus on three things that matter most. Everything else is noise.

They killed their most profitable model because it didn't serve their purpose.

The pattern is clear: every yes to purpose requires multiple nos to activity. Organizations drowning in activity are organizations that haven't learned to let go. They're trying to do everything, which guarantees they'll accomplish nothing that matters.

Purpose isn't additive. It's subtractive. What are you willing to stop doing so you can start achieving what actually matters?

Purpose-First Technology Decisions

Global AI spending reached $1.5 trillion in 2025 and is expected to blow past $2.5 trillion in 2026.[8] Yet between 70 percent and 85 percent of AI initiatives fail to deliver expected value.[9]

Why? People in organizations start with technology instead of purpose.

"We need AI strategy" shows Industrial Age checkbox thinking. Technology first, purpose second. And it's expensive as hell.

Technology Doesn't Lead. Purpose Does

Barloworld, a global leader in industrial processing, committed to digitalization in 2022. All the right elements: dedicated IT team, budget allocation, timeline, executive buy-in. Eighteen months later, minimal progress.

They'd started with technology led by IT instead of business problems.

When I began working with them, we put the digitalization strategy aside. Started with: "What's holding Barloworld back from achieving its purpose?"

The answer: increasing complexity, need for faster decision-making. Two clear issues emerged: operational efficiency in reporting and faster information delivery to internal customers. Both limiting growth, potentially costing millions annually.

Then, and only then, we explored technology solutions.

We broke it down and aligned on one specific business problem AI tools might address: consolidating accurate financial reports from 15 subsidiaries in 25 countries for board reporting. The kind of concrete challenge AI can effectively address.

Future-ready leaders don't react to "must invest in AI" pressure. They identify challenges obstructing movement toward their purpose. Then evaluate which tools help solve specific problems.

Purpose-driven organizations ask: "How can we leverage AI to accelerate toward our direction?"

Activity-driven organizations ask: "What are others doing that we should copy?"

Only one leads to competitive advantage.

When Purpose Gets Lost

I watched this happen from the inside. UB Networks, the company I still call my alma mater, built a Silicon Valley success story as a networking pioneer. I started in product marketing and moved into sales operations. It felt like family. But in the early 1990s, as connectivity needs accelerated, new technologies emerged. Routers could manage traffic intelligently, connecting multiple networks simultaneously, far beyond simple bridging.

CEO and founder Ralph Ungermann recognized the threat but decided to steer clear. He doubled down on bridges.

The purpose shifted from leading innovation to winning on product capabilities.

Jayshree Ullal saw differently. She had vision for the direction of the market. She had intuition. She wasn't set on protecting a product or hitting a KPI. She was looking at where the market was shifting next.

While senior leadership focused inward on defending what they'd built, Jayshree kept scanning. Talking to customers about their future needs, not their current purchases. Watching what competitors were building. Listening to what the market was asking for. Her confidence came from foresight, not from position.

Ralph Ungermann faced the same choice many leaders face: let go of what made him successful, or protect it until it becomes irrelevant. He chose protection. Bridges were embedded into UB Networks' identity. The board asked him to leave. The company restructured completely. New leadership literally took over our little planet. The family culture I'd loved was blown up overnight.

Jayshree understood what Ralph couldn't: in Emergence, refusing to let go of yesterday guarantees losing tomorrow. She left to follow where the market was heading. She went on to become one of the most influential leaders in networking as CEO, Arista Networks. Ralph's refusal to let go made UB Networks a footnote.

That restructuring changed my life. I negotiated a move to Europe, and my entire international career began from that single decision. Sometimes the worst thing that happens to a company can be the best thing that happens to you.

External validation expires the moment the market shifts.
Inner confidence travels with you.

This is exactly the kind of intuitive leadership future-ready navigators appreciate, someone who trusts internal knowing over external pressure, who walks away from prestigious positions when purpose gets compromised, who scans continuously rather than defending blindly.

When people drift from purpose they stop seeing possibilities and start defending positions. They optimize yesterday's solutions while tomorrow's markets emerge around them.

During a keynote in 2025, I asked 500 executives: "What's your company's purpose?" Everyone could recite something. Beautiful words they had memorized perfectly.

Then I asked: "How did that purpose influence the most important decisions you made in the past month?"

Silence. Not thoughtful pause. Uncomfortable silence. Five hundred successful leaders, and not one could name a single decision their stated purpose had actually influenced.

During my discussion with one CEO after the keynote, he admitted: "Our real purpose is meeting the board's expectations and our KPIs. Everything else is activity."

Another said: "Honestly? At this point it's just survival. I just need to make it through the year."

Exhaustion comes from pretending purpose that does not exist.

When Purpose Breaks

False purpose exhausts people.

The startup that pivots every quarter, chasing whatever venture capitalists want to fund. First "disrupting real estate through machine learning." Then "revolutionizing education with AI." Ambition without purpose. The team burns out from meaninglessness. Every pivot resets direction until direction becomes "whatever keeps us funded."

I watched one startup go through seven pivots in eighteen months. The founders could articulate each new "purpose" brilliantly: pitch decks, vision statements, team rallies. The engineers stopped believing after pivot three.

The salespeople stopped caring after pivot five. By pivot seven, people were exhausted and just going through the motions. The company still exists. The soul does not.

Leaders at corporations with beautiful purpose statements that no decision actually reflects. "Customer first" except when quarterly earnings are at risk. "Innovation matters" except when it threatens existing products. "People are our greatest asset" except during layoffs that boost stock price.

The Question That Changes Everything

The Silicon Valley question that matters: "What are you driving for or trying to achieve?" Not "What do you do or where do you work?" Purpose versus activity. That distinction changes everything.

The real question isn't whether people know their purpose or are simply displaying a nice mission statement.

It's whether they're listening to their inner voice, constantly tapping into intuition. Then, do they have the confidence to make decisions based on that purpose even when it contradicts conventional thinking, short-term profits, or stakeholder expectations?

Intuition is not the opposite of strategy.
It's where real strategy starts.

Is there real commitment to purpose? Not the statement on the wall. The kind that changes what you do on Monday morning. The kind Shantanu showed when he walked around the block instead of reaching for a spreadsheet.

Your Turn: Purpose Reflection

There's a difference between purpose that drives decisions and purpose that decorates the lobby wall.

About personal purpose:

- What energizes you regardless of recognition?
- What would you do even if it might fail?

- What's the worst that can happen? And what will it mean for your ability to achieve your purpose?
- When does work feel like contribution versus extraction?
- What impact would you create if resources weren't constrained?
- What did you want to do before you learned what you should do?

About organizational purpose:

- What decisions has your stated purpose actually changed?
- What profitable opportunities have you rejected because they didn't align?
- When did purpose cost you something significant?
- Which sacred cows would you slaughter if purpose demanded it?
- Does your purpose survive when the audience changes?

About alignment:

- Where does personal purpose conflict with organizational purpose?
- Which battles are you fighting that don't matter to your North Star?
- Who in your organization has clear purpose that doesn't fit the official one?
- What would change if everyone's actual purpose was visible?
- How much of your energy goes to performing purpose versus living it?

About navigation:

- If your current path failed, would your purpose remain?
- Which changes would strengthen your purpose versus threaten it?
- What would you stop doing immediately if purpose was your only metric?
- Who would leave if you got serious about purpose?
- Who would join?

The answers matter less than the recognition. Purpose that costs something beats purpose that sounds nice. Purpose that excludes beats purpose that tries to include everyone.

Purpose shows direction but not path. You can know exactly where you're going and still have no idea how to get there.

That's where Exploration begins, which we'll cover in the next chapter. Henry Ford didn't ask people what kind of machine they wanted. He explored what they needed to accomplish. One answer stuck: "I want to get to church faster." Not customer feedback on horse upgrades. A clear understanding of the deeper goal.

The map isn't coming. But with purpose as your North Star and exploration as your method, you don't need one.

5 Exploration: Bounded Discovery

"The real voyage of discovery consists not in seeking new landscapes, but in having new eyes."

—Marcel Proust, *In Search of Lost Time* (2023 [1913–27])

Nature understands exploration better than any strategy consultant. Years ago, biologist Pablo Borboroglu[1] found something impossible: 12 Magellanic penguins nesting in a trash heap on Argentina's coast.

The place was full of garbage, broken glass, abandoned cars, burned-out campfires. Traditional penguin colonies existed miles away on pristine beaches. These 12 had no business being there.

But they'd found something their traditional colonies lacked: abundant food sources. They didn't wait for perfect conditions. They nested in the disaster, bred successfully, and returned the next spring. Other penguins noticed. Within years, thousands of penguins were nesting there. The "trash heap" became a wildlife refuge spanning tens of thousands of acres.

The penguins teach us something essential about this inflection point: opportunity doesn't always arrive in expected forms. Sometimes the path forward runs directly through what looks like disaster.

In 1974, leaders at IKEA entered Japan confident that Swedish design and self-service would conquer another market. They'd crushed it across

Europe. The business model was bulletproof. The data screamed success. They failed spectacularly. Within months, Japanese customers rejected everything IKEA assumed would work. Japanese families considered the flat-pack furniture cheap, not clever. They found the self-service model confusing, not empowering. They thought the warehouse aesthetic looked unfinished, not modern. IKEA spent years hemorrhaging money before admitting defeat and withdrawing entirely.

The failure wasn't execution. It was lack of exploration. IKEA analyzed the Japanese market from Sweden. They studied demographics, income levels, urban density. But they never explored how Japanese families actually lived[2] or what "quality" meant in Japanese culture, why self-service felt like poor service rather than empowerment, and how compact living spaces made Swedish-sized furniture impossible.[3]

When preparing to enter Korea four decades later, IKEA spent six years exploring on the ground. They visited homes across the country, studying how families actually used their spaces and observing daily patterns.[4]

The exploration revealed what analysis couldn't: Korean families cleared furniture each night to sleep on heated floors, needed vertical storage to keep living surfaces open, and had service expectations completely different from Europe.

When IKEA finally opened in Gwangmyeong in December 2014, the store quickly became one of the company's top-performing outlets worldwide. This was dramatically different from their 12-year Japanese experiment that ended in withdrawal.[5]

The difference was exploration: exploring reality on the ground instead of studying markets from headquarters. They did not assume what worked elsewhere would work here but discovered what actually would work through real-world exploration with clear boundaries and purpose.

Purpose provided the North Star: making well-designed home furnishings accessible to everyone. But local exploration revealed the path. Without exploration, purpose remains aspiration. Without purpose, exploration becomes wandering. IKEA learned this through decades of costly failure across multiple markets.

The lesson isn't that analysis is wrong; IKEA still analyzes markets carefully. But analysis without exploration leads to very risky assumptions. And in emergence, where markets shift faster than spreadsheets update, assumptions kill companies that exploration could save. At this inflection point, where cyclones collide faster than analysis can track them, exploration becomes a survival capability.

Exploration without purpose is chaos.
Purpose without exploration is stagnation.

Paranoid Optimism

The most expensive innovation mistake is waiting for perfect knowledge that never comes.

The traditional approach is to study the market, research the competition, analyze the data, build the business case, and get committee approval. Then, maybe, carefully test something small.

That approach built the prosperity we enjoy today. Those processes weren't wrong in the Industrial Age. Right now, analysis paralysis has become more dangerous than intelligent risk-taking.

Exploration demands a different level of critical thinking than analysis. Analysis asks: what does the data say? Exploration asks: what is the data missing? Analysis seeks proof. Exploration seeks possibility. Both require critical thinking. Exploration's critical thinking questions the questions themselves.

Exploration is intentional movement toward uncertainty.

Real exploration is free and open—but only within purpose-driven boundaries. That's the paradox: boundaries don't limit exploration. They enable it. Without guardrails, exploration becomes endless wandering. With them, it becomes purposeful discovery.

Adobe didn't bet the company overnight. They tested with features offered for dimes on the dollar, learning as they went. IKEA didn't rush into South Korea—they explored the market for six years before opening a single store. Both companies gave themselves room to move, but within deliberate constraints.

The most important boundary, though, is personal—the discipline to filter out opinions, trends, and Industrial Age thinking long enough to hear your own signal. Before Adobe's transformation, Shantanu Narayen didn't go looking for answers from others. He created space for internal clarity to emerge. Whether through nature walks or simply stepping away from the noise, that practice of going inward transforms exploration from frantic activity to purposeful discovery.

Marie's daily bicycle rides through occupied territory were exploration with the tightest possible boundaries. Same purpose every day: get to work, stay alive, help who you can. But the route changed constantly. She learned which roads had new checkpoints, which roads had been bombed overnight, where patrols had shifted. She gathered intelligence not through analysis but through movement. Each ride taught her something the previous ride couldn't. That's bounded exploration. Purpose held steady. The path adapted daily based on what she discovered.

This connects directly to Purpose. Purpose shows the destination. Exploration uncovers the path. Leaders can know their purpose perfectly and still need exploration to discover how to get there. Leaders at Adobe knew they wanted to enable creativity for all. Exploration showed Narayen and the team the subscription model path.

The Comfortable Delusion

Many leaders say they need to change and hence put innovation programs in place without curiosity to really explore. While they can say they "do innovation," nothing really changes.

For them, the Industrial Age playbook still dominates:

- Hire McKinsey to analyze disruption (while disruptors build it)
- Form a "Digital Transformation Task Force" (that meets quarterly)
- Launch an "incubator" (disconnected from core business)
- Commission "Future of Work" studies (while the future arrives)
- Create innovation labs (where ideas go to die)

Meanwhile, competitors are exploring new business models in real markets, building direct customer relationships, and making decisions based on market feedback, not committee consensus.

If you're not uncomfortable, you're not moving fast enough.

The brutal reality is that companies burn up to millions of dollars in consultant fees analyzing opportunities that startups capture with $20,000 in direct market testing. Eighteen-month strategic planning cycles while market conditions change every quarter. Six-month feasibility studies for two-week experiments.

I don't care if exploration into unknown territory feels uncomfortable. Comfortable is how organizations die slowly while congratulating themselves for being careful.

They prioritize being thorough. Competitors prioritize being fast. Guess who survives?

Fear Closes What Exploration Opens

Fear tells us: "Don't try new approaches. You will fail." "Don't test that idea. It could expose weaknesses." "Don't open yourself to other perspectives. They will attack what you believe."

Closing oneself to new ideas, concepts, and the outside world feels like safety. Like prudent risk management.

It's actually the opposite.

> **Giving into the paralysis of fear closes us to exactly what we need most in emergence: new information, different perspectives, unexpected opportunities.**

People in organizations that thrive in emergence play offense. They stay open to ideas that challenge assumptions, to approaches that contradict conventional thinking, to possibilities that don't fit existing models.

This requires a different relationship with fear: recognize it, don't let it drive instinctual behavior. Feel the fear, then open up to intuition and inner clarity. Acknowledge the discomfort of fear, then explore beyond it with inner clarity.

Openness doesn't mean accepting every idea or trying every approach. It means maintaining receptivity to what's actually happening rather than defending what you wish were happening. It means listening to what the markets are telling you even when they contradict your plans. It means exploring possibilities that make you uncomfortable because that discomfort often points to opportunity, not danger.

IKEA's losses in Japan came from leaders closing, refusing to see that their assumptions didn't match market reality. Their Korea success came from opening, exploring what customers actually wanted rather than defending what IKEA thought they should want.

That choice determines survival.

The Paranoia That Creates Progress

Andy Grove, Intel's legendary CEO, understood something many leaders still miss: "Only the paranoid survive." Not only paranoid about competition copying products, paranoid about assumptions becoming obsolete.

Grove built Intel into a semiconductor giant by constantly looking outside, scanning the market and questioning what could kill the company. Not next year. Next quarter. This systematic paranoia drove Intel to explore continuously, cannibalize their own products before competitors could, and pivot from memory chips to microprocessors when the market shifted in a move that seemed insane but saved the company.

This is awareness. At this inflection point, where AI transforms industries in months and consumer preferences shift overnight, Grove's paranoia becomes survival requirement for everyone. The question isn't whether markets will shift. The question is whether people in organizations are exploring fast enough to see it coming.

Amazon: Exploration as Operating System

Leaders with an Industrial Age mindset treat exploration as a periodic initiative or a separate place (innovation labs, incubators). Leaders of future-ready companies like Amazon embed exploration into daily operations as competitive advantage.

Amazon doesn't wait for annual planning cycles. Innovation is continuous, with multiple exploration loops running simultaneously. When customers repeatedly request a capability, teams explore it immediately—not in next quarter's roadmap. New services launch based on patterns in real customer usage, not projections from a boardroom.

The exploration rhythm is relentless. A customer request on Monday triggers deeper exploration by Wednesday. A prototype emerges the following week. A new service launches within months. While competitors are still debating whether to explore cloud services, Amazon has already launched, learned, and iterated three times over.

But this isn't chaos—it's systematic responsiveness. Every exploration is filtered through clear questions: will customers use it? Will they pay for it? Does it advance the platform? Rapid testing delivers real answers faster than any feasibility study ever could.

This is what continuous exploration looks like in practice—and it exposes the fatal flaw in traditional planning cycles. By the time legacy organizations finish their analysis, customers have already moved on. Often to a competitor that was willing to explore first and refine later.

All of this serves Amazon's purpose: to be Earth's most customer-centric company. That's not a tagline—it's the engine behind their exploration obsession. At Amazon, refusing to explore means refusing to listen to customers. And refusing to listen to customers isn't a strategic misstep. It's an identity violation.

Whatever you think of Jeff Bezos or Amazon's market dominance, the lesson here isn't about the man or the machine. It's about what happens when an organization anchors every decision—every experiment, every failure, every pivot—to a purpose clear enough to act on. That kind of clarity is available to any leader willing to define it.

Making Exploration Practical

Exploration generates possibilities. But without purpose-driven guardrails, it becomes tourism. Small tests generate real learning.

Start with One "What If?" Adobe didn't explore impact of changing their entire business model at once. They started with one solution—Photoshop, asking users one question: "What features are most important to you NOW?" Not twenty questions. One question, tested broadly.

After two weeks asking this to thousands of customers globally, they explored offering three new capabilities and returned to customers with the next question. "What are you willing to pay to use this for a month?"

Breaking the unknown down into focused questions or areas for exploration speeds the process and provides validation without massive risk. Each small exploration builds confidence for the next, creating momentum through discovery rather than paralysis through analysis.

Time Boundaries Create Urgency Every successful exploration has defined endpoints. Adobe's teams reconvened every few days. Later in this chapter, you'll meet a young cancer survivor whose various three-month discovery phases transformed his future. IKEA's Korean experiment ran six years with clear milestones. Without boundaries, exploration becomes endless wandering that produces nothing.

From Study Tours to Real Engagement People stuck in Industrial Age mindset rituals such as study tours to see innovation in action, review PowerPoint presentations from consultants and create benchmarking reports that gather dust. Budget money gets spent yet nothing is created.

Future-ready innovation results from hands-on engagement. Jump into the sandbox and get dirty. Learn, challenge, and experience using new approaches.

Make exploration part of each day, not a quarterly event.

Run weekly learning labs where teams experience different large language models (LLMs) addressing real business challenges. Launch 48-hour sprints that solve actual company problems with real constraints. Replace the quarterly customer satisfaction survey with one customer conversation per day. Ship minimum viable products (MVPs) to learn this week rather than planning for perfection forever.

> ***The unique power of Silicon Valley has never been just speed—it's the collective insight that emerges when people of diverse perspectives explore together. A developer from Brazil, a designer from Denmark, and a customer rep from Detroit in a Learning Lab, all wrestling with the same core question: what if?***
>
> ***This combination—continual exploration, diverse perspectives, and a shared willingness to try whatever it takes to reach the purpose—is what turns innovation from a quarterly initiative into a daily practice. Not in months. Not in years but in days.***

Google: When Brilliance Isn't Enough

Around 2012, Google faced a strategic inflection point. Android had just surpassed iOS. International ad revenues were overtaking US results. The company needed to scale its global presence—fast. But the question wasn't simply about expansion. It was about relevance: how does a company built in Mountain View truly serve consumers and business leaders across Asia-Pacific, Latin America, Europe, the Middle East, and Africa?

I and Next Step were engaged to address the question of "what can we do now to scale our successful model into new markets?" Unlike traditional consulting firms, we didn't start with market research. We started with purpose. What does meaningful presence in Asia-Pacific actually look like? What does success in Latin America mean for Google's broader vision? That clarity drove exploration—but not the comfortable kind.

Working alongside Google's teams, we helped them go directly to the markets themselves. Not to validate assumptions, but to challenge them. What trust meant in São Paulo was different from what it meant in Singapore. How commerce worked in Lagos bore little resemblance to how it worked in London. The patterns Google expected to find weren't there.

The exploration surfaced hard realities. Messaging had to change by region. Business models needed fundamental adaptation. What worked in Mountain View often didn't translate. Even brilliant leaders with exceptional teams can build echo chambers without realizing it—and Google's teams discovered they had blind spots they couldn't see from the inside.

Throughout, our role wasn't to deliver products. It was to facilitate better questions, challenge assumptions, and connect Google's leaders directly with the markets they intended to serve. They explored and learned by doing—through engagement with partners, suppliers, and customers in country.

The result went beyond any single market strategy. Google's leaders developed the capability to navigate unfamiliar territory themselves. When the next market emerged, they didn't need to repeat the process from scratch. They had learned how to explore—by first learning to listen to people who see the world differently than they do.

The more important question is this: if exploration delivers results like that, why do even the sharpest leaders default to what they already know?

Google is one of the most innovative companies on the planet, staffed with some of the sharpest minds in technology. And yet they still had to be pushed to go beyond taking familiar actions. This isn't a Google problem. It's a human one—and the explanation is literally in our heads.

How Your Brain Explores Action

The science is neurological. When leaders see an opportunity, they are ready to act based on what they know at the moment. The brain defaults to the substantia nigra, the region that craves familiar rewards and known results. The prefrontal cortex, the largest part of our brain, responsible for creative problem-solving and breakthrough thinking, gets hijacked by threat detection. To the amygdala every unknown becomes a danger to avoid rather than an opportunity to explore. See Figure 2.1.

When people shift to believing exploration then action creates certainty, the prefrontal cortex stays engaged. The brain starts pattern-matching for possibilities instead of scanning for reasons to wait. It calculates opportunities instead of risks.

Grove's paranoia paradoxically creates courage. When people accept that standing still is the real threat, exploration becomes the safe choice. The brain stops protecting the status quo and starts pursuing the possible.

This connects directly to Chapter 2 on biology working against the emergence mindset. The same neural pathways that resist "not knowing" also resist exploration. Purposeful exploration can override the brain's preference for familiar patterns, just as intuition can override expertise paralysis. In emergence, future-ready leaders who override biological resistance to uncertainty gain decisive advantage.

When Exploration Bypasses Structure

Sometimes exploration—both internal and external—reveals that the structures, habits, and patterns people cling to aren't actually necessary. They never were.

Dave Morgan discovered this in an Austrian pub in 1965.

As a University of Toronto student struggling with French and German, Dave enrolled in a summer program in Salzburg. One night he found himself sitting between two men who didn't share a common language—a

German from Dortmund and a Frenchman from Lyon. After about three liters of beer, something unexpected happened. Dave realized he was translating German to French and French to German—without routing anything through English.

The beer didn't create the ability. It quieted the part of his brain that insisted translation had to follow proper channels. The capability had always been there. Exploration simply revealed it.

That single discovery shaped Dave's entire career. He became, in his words, "rapidly redeployable, able to go up a learning curve very quickly"—not through formal credentials but through recognizing that his brain could bypass traditional structures when it was allowed to. His dream of becoming an international management consultant didn't materialize through the path he planned. Top consulting firms wouldn't even interview him. It materialized through what emerged when he stopped forcing a route and stayed open to discovery.

Most organizations never have that moment in the pub. They force everything through their lens—through headquarters, through hierarchy, through established process. Every insight, every decision, every innovation routed through channels that feel necessary but may have been optional all along.

Exploration reveals buried pathways that have already existed. Future-ready leaders are those who let go of corporate-first patterns.

The Speed Cyclone that destroyed established music distribution didn't go through traditional channels—it was a 20-year-old hitting the wrong button to launch Napster. Neither does AI, which exploded over night with the unplanned release of ChatGPT. At today's inflection point when Speed meets Pressure and collides with Humanity, industries become obsolete overnight.

"Yes and" Thinking

The shift from analysis to exploration expands the opportunities.

Industrial Age organizations mastered thorough preparation: detailed market research, comprehensive competitive analysis, risk assessment matrices. This systematic approach built global enterprises, created millions of jobs, and generated unprecedented prosperity. These methods remain invaluable for certain contexts such as building bridges, developing pharmaceuticals, managing nuclear facilities. When failure has catastrophic consequences, thorough analysis before action saves lives.

But at this inflection point, emergence demands something additional: the ability to learn through experiencing and doing things that are uncomfortable when perfect information doesn't exist. When customer preferences shift overnight, when new competitors emerge from unexpected sectors, waiting for complete analysis means missing the opportunity entirely.

Three common questions I get from Nordic CEOs are: "Is there a role for our tenured research analysts?" and "Should we implement additional AI analytical tools?" and "Do we need to keep investing in innovation initiatives?"

My answer is "it depends."

Rigorous analysis led by tenured experts has its place ***and*** the latest AI tools will amplify their discoveries. The results of people with technology need to be used in innovative spin-outs.

This is Silicon Valley 1 + 1 = 3 thinking: by combining approaches, solutions, and initiatives, people in future-ready organizations create greater collective value than either can achieve alone.

The Industrial Age beliefs, structures, and companies led us to the world we live in today. Global healthcare systems. Infrastructure that connects continents. Education that shifted literacy from privilege to expectation.

That's not nothing. That's extraordinary. And the question isn't whether the Industrial Age was right—it was right, for its conditions. The question is what still serves us now that those conditions have fundamentally changed.

This is where critical thinking becomes essential. Not as an academic exercise, but as a personal one. What learning from the Industrial Age still serves your purpose? What needs letting go? And what happens when you combine the best of Industrial Age experience with AI capabilities and entirely new approaches to move forward now?

The answer isn't abandoning what worked. It isn't blindly adopting what's new. It's having the clarity to draw from everything available—*and the courage to leave the rest behind.*

That sounds like philosophy. For some people, it's lived experience.

Comfort with ambiguity isn't a personality trait. It's a survival skill. And sometimes it's forged in circumstances no one would choose.

Comfort with ambiguity isn't a personality trait.
It's a survival skill.

Kristian had spent two years battling cancer. At 18, when he completed secondary school and peers were starting university, he was healthy and ready to think about his future. But the time in treatment had set him back.

"I've already lost two years of exploration," he told his school counsellor. "I need to make them up quickly to gain experience so I can figure out my future direction."

The counselor's suggestion was sensible: research universities, talk to people in leadership positions, take some time to travel, then apply for the program that will prepare you for a stable career. The Industrial Age playbook for life planning.

Kristian's answer was, "I don't have time for that. I need to gain real experience now to decide on the right actions to take at year end."

Instead of doing endless research, Kristian built his own exploration plan:

1. Try out entrepreneurship through launching an online business
2. Experience consumer-facing opportunities through working in a traditional storefront while volunteering at the local hospital
3. Complete an AI coding bootcamp
4. Build relationships, ask questions, work with mentor who brings decades of corporate experience

At each stage of his exploration journey, he asked: does this energize me? Does it connect to something bigger than myself? Can this help me achieve my real purpose?

As Kristian learned throughout the year, his greatest insights came from his intuition. By always questioning, listening to what felt right and going internal for clarity of the possible impact of each discovery, he turned exploration into commitment for today into the future.

Intuition as Navigation Guide

I was at DataTrak, a small software company in Mountain View, with about 60 employees. The CEO, Ed, was getting married and needed to sell his apartment in Redwood City. I had 70 percent of my down payment saved; Ed arranged a bridge loan through the company for the rest. I closed on Friday.

That weekend was a company offsite with strategy sessions and celebration of previous quarter's results. Monday morning, I had flown to Michigan, meeting with a prospect when Ed called. He'd sold the company to Software Shop Systems on the East Coast. No warning. No discussion. My role as channel sales manager, gone. I was in my twenties.

I didn't wait but immediately started exploring roles within the acquiring company and elsewhere.

My purpose then was not to change the world. It was to survive. Pay the mortgage. Not be homeless. It was very specific and tangible.

I stayed on nine long months commuting from Redwood City to New Jersey, before letting go and joining a Silicon Valley startup. Within six months, they ran out of money. My Wells Fargo account balance: minus $27. Every bit of my savings was in that apartment, with a huge mortgage.

Instinct said panic, logic said sell the apartment. But intuition said I belonged in it. I secured roommates, sold my jewelry, lived on rice and beans. I had inner clarity that I would find ways to pay the mortgage and a new job.

A few months later, Ungermann-Bass found me—or maybe I found it. Either way, it was the spark.

Listening to intuition, sometimes called "going internal," is a necessity at today's Emergence inflection point. While everything accelerates externally, going internal creates the stillness where clarity emerges. A different kind of intelligence. The gut processing patterns your conscious mind misses. The heart's knowing that transcends logic.

Gen Zs do this naturally. They step away from a project to check in with themselves. They take mental health days to gain energy. They understand that going internal is navigation. Their parents burned out from constant external focus. This generation learned that sustainable exploration requires regular internal reflection.

Reflection transforms exploration from random activity to systematic learning. After coming through this experience, I reflected: what really happened? What did I feel throughout the journey? What worked? What felt right and aligned with purpose?

The DataTrak experience tested my inner confidence, resilience, and adaptability and strengthened my commitment to truly make a difference in the world. It also taught me to take life one day at time with the inner confidence that I can navigate whatever the cyclones throw at me.

AI as Your Scout

Reflection creates the clarity. Now the question becomes: how do you act on it faster, smarter, and at a scale no individual mind could achieve alone? The answer isn't more analysis or bigger committees. It's knowing how to use the right tools—and using them with the judgment that only human experience and self-awareness can provide. This is where AI comes in.

AI is simply a tool, like a kitchen knife. Essential for a chef preparing a meal, dangerous if used carelessly, harmful if wielded with bad intent. The tool isn't good or evil; the application determines the result.

If you take all the best, sharpest knives and put them in a room filled with killers, catastrophe happens. That's simply not smart. Put the best knives in the hands of the chefs, and there are fewer knives for the killers to get hold of. I believe 95 percent of people on this planet are of positive intent. We have a moral duty to use AI tools and train them positively. Because if we don't, the negative actors will win.

Right now, AI exploration separates future-ready people from those stuck analyzing while competitors act.

Many people approach AI backwards. They hire armies of consultants or a chief AI officer to explore the right tools, commit investment to one "safe" tool such as Copilot and announce "we are using AI," all before understanding what problems they're trying to solve. That's like buying every knife in the store before knowing what meal to cook.

Rushing to implement AI without exploration fails spectacularly. The 70–90 percent failure rate for AI initiatives isn't because the technology doesn't work. It's because people in organizations skip the exploration phase entirely. They don't test multiple tools to understand differences. They don't explore what problems AI actually solves versus what problems it creates. They don't ask people experiencing the work what would genuinely help.

The exploration question isn't "How do we implement AI?" but "What is the greatest challenge we are not able to solve?"

Van Ameyde: The Question That Changed Everything

The European insurance claims processor had a problem—actually, three.

Forty-five minutes per claim with seven-week backlogs. This led to 80 percent annual turnover of customer service representatives (CSRs).

Most leaders would have asked: how do we make this faster? Van Ameyde's leaders asked something more fundamental: what if humans shouldn't be doing this work at all?

That single question opened the exploration.

They found an AI tool built specifically for insurance claims processing. What took exhausted CSRs 45 minutes to complete, the system handled in three—often more accurately. The 150-person team became 30 people focused exclusively on the work requiring human judgment: complex disputes, unusual cases, the relationships no algorithm can replace.

But Van Ameyde didn't stop at efficiency. While the technology was being tested, leaders sat down with every CSR and asked: what energizes you? What work gives you a sense of purpose? Then they rebuilt roles, training, and workflows based on the answers. Customer relationship management for those who came alive in human connection. Deep analysis for those energized by problem-solving. Innovation for those who wanted to create what didn't yet exist.

The results after three years speak for themselves. Turnover dropped from 80 percent to 2 percent. Average tenure grew from five months to more than two years. Customer satisfaction soared, resulting in revenue growth.

This is what future-ready AI exploration actually looks like—not rushing to implement technology for Industrial Age efficiency, but redesigning the organization around humanity plus AI so people are engaged doing what humans should be doing in the first place.

The technology didn't transform Van Ameyde. The question of "what should people be doing" did.

How Netflix Used AI to Solve One Problem

Prior to COVID 19, Netflix faced a specific, commercially brutal challenge: engagement. People were signing up, but many were not watching enough. And Netflix knew one thing with certainty: the more members watched, the longer they stayed subscribed. The less they watched, the faster they cancelled. Simple equation. Massive revenue impact.

Rather than trying to optimize everything at once (content creation, pricing, interface design, or marketing) Netflix leveraged AI to address a single, high-leverage problem: identifying patterns and directing people to something they actually wanted to watch.[6]

Netflix used machine learning to analyze behavior at scale. Not just ratings, but what people really did: what they binged, what they abandoned, how long they browsed without clicking, what time of day they watched, and how viewing patterns changed by context. The system learned that the same person might prefer crime documentaries on weekend evenings and light romantic comedies after work during the week. Preferences were situational, not fixed.[7]

This behavioral insight enabled a shift from generic recommendations to deep personalization. Netflix moved beyond "people who watched X also watched Y" to surfacing content that fit a specific person in a specific moment. Even the artwork shown for a single title became personalized, with different thumbnails displayed to different users based on what was most likely to attract them.[8]

The impact was material. Netflix has stated that personalized recommendations drive more than 80 percent of all viewing on the platform. Increased viewing directly supported retention, reducing churn by helping members quickly find content they enjoyed. What began as a clear use of AI to solve a strategic problem became one of Netflix's most durable competitive advantages.[9]

The key wasn't AI. It was using technology to expand exploration of patterns, behaviors, and hypotheses beyond what people could do on their own. Netflix used AI to address one problem with one focus and a measurable outcome.

AI for Scale, Humans for Strategy

Pharma companies from Novartis to AstraZeneca and Moderna use AI to accelerate drug discovery. The challenge: analyzing millions of patient diagnoses, reactions, and test results that humans physically can't process at scale.

Success is the result of the critical thinking—by the people leading the research. They identify the datasets that matter, the patterns to investigate, testing sequences, how to design trials. AI does what humans can't: synthesizing broad datasets, identifying reaction patterns across thousands of patients, tracking real-time responses during trials.

This frees researchers from laboratory details to collaborate directly with patients and healthcare providers for input. Faster research cycles, leading-edge analysis tools, and direct patient engagement combine to compress drug development timelines from decades to years.

Suresh, working with Novartis in the oncology team, lives this daily. He validates the critical questions for cancer prevention while using AI to analyze patient data patterns. His focus on purpose and critical thinking determines what, where, and how to investigate the data. AI's processing power makes exploration possible at scale.

Real AI platform exploration means trying at least three different approaches, not to pick the "best" one but to understand what trade-offs each makes. One tool prioritizes speed. Another prioritizes accuracy. A third balances both but requires more setup. You learn these differences through bounded exploration: small tests, clear criteria, actual use.

People in organizations succeeding with AI explore like scientists rather than implement like engineers. They explore hypotheses. Then compare results and critically question assumptions. Future-ready navigators learn what works through doing, not through planning.

The AI Paradox Nobody Talks About

Effective use of AI takes *more* time and *more* brain power than not using AI.

Using AI well means engaging the prefrontal cortex intensively, the most energy-expensive part of the brain. Asking "What if?", comparing outputs, questioning assumptions, synthesizing information: these are cognitively demanding tasks. AI handles routine cognitive work (substantia nigra territory), but using it effectively requires serious prefrontal cortex engagement. Brain-intensive work. Getting good results from AI comes down to three things: context, specificity, and guardrails. (The appendix walks through each in detail.)

Consultants rarely mention this. Future-ready leaders live it.

When Jensen Huang, NVIDIA's CEO, uses generative AI, he never trusts a single output.[10] He uses three or more different tools (Claude, ChatGPT, Gemini), asks each the same question, and then analyzes why the answers differ.[11] Where does truth actually lie? What assumptions is each tool making? What context is missing?[12] Exploring multiple perspectives is more thorough. It is also more intelligent, more demanding, and definitely not faster.

The promise that AI enables "doing more with less" misses the point entirely. The Emergence reality is that AI enables deeper thinking about what actually matters, for those willing to do the brain-intensive work.

Building Exploration Discipline: Curiosity and Creativity Unleashed

Systematic exploration isn't random experimentation. It's disciplined discovery with clear elements: purpose guiding direction. Questions needing answers. Timelines for decisions. Criteria for evaluation. Perspectives bringing different views.

Many young professionals already operate this way. They'll launch a TikTok campaign to test an idea rather than commission research. They'll build and ship rather than analyze and delay. They believe real-world feedback over theoretical projections. They've seen too many perfect plans fail while scrappy experiments succeed.

Making exploration practical means starting tomorrow, not next quarter. Going internal for clarity, then external for validation. Acting on inner knowing while gathering outer evidence.

Successful exploration requires two fundamental shifts: from knowing to questioning (curiosity) and from following to creating (creativity).

Curiosity: The Questions That Open Possibilities

Active questioning that challenges assumptions. For Adobe, curiosity means asking customers directly rather than assuming their preferences. At IKEA, it meant wondering why Japanese customers were not buying, then discovering fundamental misunderstandings about living spaces and service expectations.

Real curiosity requires humility. Admitting that despite success in twenty countries, what works in Sweden might fail in Korea. Acknowledging that decades of experience do not guarantee understanding of emerging markets. Recognizing that the newest employee will see opportunities that senior leadership misses.

Future-ready leaders build curiosity into culture. Regular "What if?" sessions. What if the biggest assumption is wrong? What if customers want the opposite of what the team is building? What if there is a completely different way to solve this problem? Testable hypotheses that drive exploration.

Creativity: Thinking Beyond Established Patterns

Creativity in exploration means looking in unexpected places, combining what others separate, questioning what others accept.

Creativity multiplies when different perspectives collide. A Vietnamese intern sees opportunities that a 50-year-old Swedish executive misses. Different lenses, different insights. Strategic exploration brings these perspectives together as equals.

Future-ready leaders spend time with young people: kids, teenagers, the next generation. They see what experience has trained others to overlook. They question what others have learned to accept. IKEA's reverse mentoring (Gen Z mentoring 50-year-old executives) is leadership development, providing new insights and market intelligence. The leaders who learn fastest will be those humble enough to listen to people who have never known the past.

Focus on purpose is essential because it shows ***how*** to actually explore: through curiosity and creativity.

Your Turn: Exploration Reflection

Sit with these for a few minutes. Be honest.

What's actually happening:

- What assumption about the business could be tested this week?
- Where has curiosity been replaced by certainty?

- What "What if?" question would transform the industry?
- Who sees the organization through completely different eyes?

About exploration barriers:

- Where is analysis paralysis preventing real learning?
- What could be discovered through a 48-hour exploration?
- Which sacred cow needs challenging through exploration?
- When did the organization last discover something surprising?

About AI and human potential:

- How will AI free people to do more meaningful work?
- What human capacity wants to emerge if repetitive work disappeared?
- Where could technology amplify rather than replace human creativity?

About personal exploration:

- What would you explore if failure wasn't possible?
- Which certainty will actually be assumption?
- What energizes you that the organization doesn't know about?

Exploration without action is just tourism. Leaders at Adobe explored what customers would pay for. Success came from actually launching. Leaders at IKEA explored Korean homes for six years. Profitability came from opening stores.

Those who move while others analyze define what is possible.

6 Action: Act, Ask, Iterate, Repeat

"In any moment of decision, the best thing you can do is the right thing, the next best thing is the wrong thing, and the worst thing you can do is nothing."

—Theodore Roosevelt

With more than 40 percent of the US smartphone market at its peak, BlackBerry had everything needed to dominate smartphones. Then the iPhone launched in June 2007.

They chose analysis over action.[1]

The timeline tells the story:

- 2007: iPhone launches. Co-CEO of Blackberry Jim Balsillie refers to it as "one more entrant driving this high growth space." BlackBerry's worldwide market share actually keeps growing, hitting nearly 20 percent by 2009. Leadership sees touchscreens as a fad. Physical keyboards are "what business users demand."
- 2008: Co-CEO Mike Lazaridis declares: "The most exciting mobile trend is full Qwerty keyboards. It really is. I'm not making this up." Meanwhile, Apple launches the App Store. Android releases its first phone. BlackBerry releases the Storm, its "big touchscreen" response, to terrible reviews.

- 2011: BlackBerry's worldwide market share drops below 9 percent while Android surges past 50 percent. The company lays off thousands and delays its next-generation platform repeatedly.
- 2016: BlackBerry's market share hits 0.0 percent. They exit hardware completely.[2]

The financial destruction: stock price collapsed from its peak of $147.55 to under $15, a 90 percent decline. Fourth quarter 2016, BlackBerry sold 207,900 devices in total. Market share: 0.048 percent. Thousands of jobs lost. They didn't just lose the smartphone market, they lost the chance to lead the mobile revolution.[3]

BlackBerry didn't lack capability. They had superior keyboard technology, unmatched email security, and enterprise relationships competitors envied. They didn't lack intelligence. They had brilliant engineers, and internal documents show they understood touchscreen potential, app ecosystem importance, and consumer market growth.

They lacked commitment and a willingness to let go of their plans, presumptions, and previous success.

BlackBerry's failure teaches the most critical lesson about action in emergence: letting go is not optional. Letting go of what made you successful. Letting go of identity tied to yesterday's wins. The physical keyboard was not just a product feature. It was BlackBerry's identity, their differentiator, their pride. Letting go would mean admitting their expertise no longer mattered. So they clung to keyboards while the world moved to touchscreens. They chose the certainty of slow death over the uncertainty of transformation.

While they studied touchscreens, Apple sold millions. While they debated consumer features, Android captured the mass market. Everyone, including enterprise clients, moved to iPhone and Android.

The cruel lesson: BlackBerry's hesitation didn't reduce risk, it guaranteed failure. Billions in lost market value.[4] Thousands of jobs destroyed. Market leadership evaporated. All because they mistook analysis for action.

Action beats analysis when the world is changing faster than your slide deck.

Right now, hesitation while the cyclones collide is corporate suicide.

Analysis Paralysis

Waiting for more information feels responsible. It isn't. While people in organizations analyze markets, competitors capture them. While committees debate possibilities, customers choose alternatives. While leaders wait for certainty that emergence will never provide, the window closes. Analysis paralysis doesn't reduce risk. It guarantees obsolescence.

This organizational disease destroys more innovation than any external competitor ever could. The symptoms spread through corporate culture like a virus.

It starts with best intentions. Market opportunity emerges. Customer needs shift. New technology creates possibilities. Leadership recognizes potential and does what is responsible: "Let's run a pilot to test this before we commit."

It is purely Industrial Age thinking: sequential, risk-averse, externally validated.

What follows is an elaborate ritual which consumes years of organizational energy while producing zero market results.

The pattern is consistent: Phase 1: "Let's explore this opportunity. Need to understand the market better." Phase 2: "The pilot shows promise. Let's continue it with more variables." Phase 3: "Learning a lot. Let's expand it to validate assumptions." Phase 4: "Results are mixed. Need to refine approach and test again." Phase 5: "Market seems to be shifting. Let's close the pilot."

All this across a three-year period. Each phase feels reasonable in isolation. Each decision seems prudent. Each delay appears justified by complexity, risk management, and due diligence.

Resources get trapped. People and budgets are consumed with evaluation instead of killing or scaling innovation.

Future-ready people don't want to run explorations forever. They want to build things that matter.

Every month spent perfecting a pilot is a month competitors spend learning from actual customers.

Opportunities have expiration dates. Windows close. By the time the pilot has been proven, the time to act has passed by.

Teams get demoralized. Nothing destroys momentum like projects that never launch. When piloting becomes a permanent state, the best talent seeks places where work reaches real customers.

Meanwhile, future-ready creators bypass the pilot. They launch businesses overnight from the basement. Build audiences on Instagram. While committees debate digital strategy, they are already iterating version three based on real customer feedback.

A pilot program is often just a polite way of staying paralyzed. Marie didn't "pilot" surrendering at the bridge; she didn't ask the soldiers to move one piece of debris to see what happened. She went all in. In emergence, a "pilot" without a commitment to scale is just expensive procrastination. If you aren't prepared to fail completely, you are simply performing—not actively producing.

> *Marie's life proves purpose doesn't require pilots. Cycling to the air force base through enemy territory, caring for war survivors—she had one chance to act. Each day, she reflected, listened to her intuition, adjusted her route, and moved forward.*
>
> *Today, as the cyclones swirl, future-ready leaders do the same—moving from exploration to reality.*

The Classroom Has Left the Building

Marie's story isn't ancient history—it's a blueprint. The same instinct that carried her through enemy territory is the instinct that separates leaders who talk about transformation from those who deliver it. Purpose, clarity, and the courage to move without a guaranteed outcome. That readiness doesn't happen by accident. It gets built through action.

Most of us didn't choose our mental models. They were handed to us—in rows, under fluorescent lights, by a system designed to produce predictable outputs from unpredictable human beings. Before we can build future-ready organizations, we have to understand why so many leaders default to compliance, caution, and control. It starts much earlier than the boardroom—in the classroom.

Education is not broken because students stopped caring. It is broken because the model was built for a world that no longer exists.

The traditional classroom was designed for Industrial Age compliance—sit still, absorb what the teacher delivers, reproduce it on command, wait your turn. That worked when employers needed people who could follow instructions on a factory floor or execute predictable processes in a cubicle. That world is gone.

During Emergence, learning happens through experience—through exploration, experimentation, failure, iteration, and creation. Not through passive consumption of content someone else decided was relevant. The most important skills in today's workplace cannot be taught from the front of a room. They must be lived.

And Gen Z knows it.

Ninety-three percent of Gen Z knowledge workers use two or more AI tools per week—not because their professors assigned it, but because they are wired for exploration over instruction. They try things, learn fast, iterate, and move forward before committees finish their second meeting. They aren't waiting for permission. They're building the future while institutions are still drafting the policy.

Yet many educators, operating from an Industrial Age mindset are blocking it, because they see technology as a threat. Banning AI tools in classrooms doesn't prepare students for a world where AI fluency is a baseline job requirement. It guarantees their disadvantage on day one.

Some institutions are getting this right. My alma mater, San José State University, is one of approximately 130 universities now recognized as Creative Campus AI adopters, partnering with companies like Adobe to place emerging tools directly in the hands of students and faculty. The philosophy is the same one I encountered there decades ago.

Don't wait until you're ready—get ready by starting.

My San José State professors delivered great programs—from their front line experience as entrepreneurs, investors, leaders before the perfect curricula existed. Faculty and students explored together. Coursework led us students into corporate assignments, learning, delivering, and advancing. That is not recklessness. That is Emergence in action.

Gen Z Isn't Waiting for Permission

The signal from Gen Z goes deeper than technology. When 86 percent say purpose is critical to job satisfaction—and 44 percent have already turned down employers based on ethical misalignment—they are not being idealistic.[5] They are being strategic. They watched what happened to their parents: decades following the Industrial Age playbook of patient climbing and perfect preparation, only to be laid off in downturns, or burned out chasing metrics that meant nothing. The lesson landed hard: waiting for certainty is a path to obsolescence.

Future-ready education doesn't teach students what to think. It builds their capacity to explore, create, collaborate, and lead through uncertainty—with AI as a partner, not a threat. That is the only curriculum that matters now.

Why Hesitation Feels Safe but Guarantees Failure

In Emergence, waiting ***is*** the risk.

As Chapter 2 revealed, hesitation comes from biology. The brain detecting uncertainty, signalling potential danger. The amygdala fires faster than thought when facing the unknown. The substantia nigra craves familiar patterns, rewarding repetition over risk. But when hesitation hardens into paralysis, biology becomes a barrier.

People tell themselves they're being prudent by preserving options, avoiding mistakes. They're actually choosing irrelevance in slow motion. Each "let's wait and see" lets someone else create the future.

The damage happens gradually, which makes it seductive. Competitors try something new while others wait for data. Markets shift while strategies get perfected. Every hesitation creates small gaps that compound into chasms.

BlackBerry's leader thought they were being responsible. They thought they were protecting shareholder value. They thought they were managing risk carefully. But the biggest risk in emergence is hesitating while markets transform, competitors advance, and opportunities expire.

Purpose without action remains philosophy. North Stars don't get closer through contemplation. Exploration without action is expensive tourism: fascinating to discuss, worthless for reaching destination.

The real question: can you afford ***not*** to act?

Future-ready leaders are moving ahead while traditional organizations are stuck in the wrong era.

Industrial Age: Perfect Before Progress

Traditional organizations still operate on a core belief: perfect planning prevents problems. They spend months defining, testing, and perfecting each approach. Risk avoidance is critical.

While there is value in risk mitigation, the result is often 18-month strategic planning cycles for 3-month market windows, six-figure consulting studies for five-figure problems, committee consensus for individual decisions, and risk matrices that measure everything except opportunity cost.

The Industrial Age created prosperity through this approach. When markets were stable, competition predictable, and change measurable in decades, thorough preparation made sense.

Silicon Valley: Move Fast, Break Things

While building, transforming, and integrating Silicon Valley companies, I am continually reminded that perfect is the enemy of progress.

In 2006, while Blackberry was at its peak, I led the market launch of the Handspring TREO—the first touchscreen smartphone integrating internet, email, phone, and calendar on an easy to use handheld device. After a 12-month design to development period, it had bugs. But 90 percent of the time, it worked brilliantly.

Within hours of launch, the production team was working overtime to keep up with demand. As RIM was perfecting Qwerty keyboards, Handspring proved the power of touchscreen interaction with mobile apps synchronized with business tools.

From a Silicon Valley perspective, "Why not?" outperforms strategic planning. Every move forward is an opportunity—to learn, succeed, or fail—fast.

Emergence: Purpose-Driven Action

Future-ready leaders learn from the Industrial Age when precision matters. They apply Silicon Valley speed when markets shift rapidly and first-mover advantage counts. But Emergence requires something neither approach offers alone: purpose as a compass.

Explore alternatives with discipline. Then choose—not the perfect option, but the one that moves you toward purpose. Act on it this week. Ask for feedback, check impact, adjust. Don't study why, just adjust and reiterate.

The real Emergence question: *what action can I take this week to move closer to my purpose?*

Action generates learning which creates insight. Insight enables better action. This is purposeful momentum—not the frantic motion of fear, but forward movement driven by inner clarity navigation leading to the North Star.

Methodology Versus Mindset

As the cyclones began spinning in the 2000s, "Agile" became "cool."

The irony is painful. Agility means responsiveness, adaptation, learning through movement. But "Agile methodology" often creates new rigidity. Teams follow sprint ceremonies religiously while missing market signals. They improve velocity metrics while customers abandon products. They perfect their process while purpose gets lost.

True agility isn't a methodology. It's a mindset. It means responding to reality rather than following process. It means changing direction when purpose demands it, not when the sprint ends. It means thinking critically about what serves the North Star, not blindly following prescribed practices.

Real agility isn't speed. It's the confidence to pivot when reality shifts.

My keynote for the EuroFinance International conference in Vienna in 2022[6] was entitled "How Fragile Is Agile." I stood in front of a room full of senior finance and treasury leaders, all invested in Agile transformation programs, all nodding along to sprint plans and stakeholder engagement models. The benefits seemed obvious: break complex projects into manageable pieces, engage stakeholders, measure progress through peer-reviewed processes.

Then I asked what they were actually achieving. Agile programs that succeeded on paper delivering short-term objectives while missing the strategic problem entirely. Sprints producing minimum viable products that became technical debt instead of robust solutions were great examples of methodology delivering the opposite of agility.

The real question isn't whether you have an Agile Program. It's whether your leaders, teams, and business are agile.

Over decades I've experienced both versions. Teams that with an agile mindset delivering small iterations, gaining feedback, and rapidly adjusting without ever calling it Agile. I have also seen teams that followed every Agile certification step perfectly while remaining completely rigid in thinking.

The difference? Mindset and confidence from internal clarity versus external validation.

Teams with true agility have confidence in their intuition and judgment. Their inner clarity guides their actions as they move beyond exploration toward their purpose. Sometimes they run sprints, gather feedback in war rooms as they navigate. Their guts and nervous systems tell them what is needed faster than analysis can. Neurological agility, responding to human intelligence and intuition, is what makes them future-ready.

Action in Emergence demands an agile mindset. Not methodology masquerading as flexibility. Real responsiveness to what's actually happening.

Perfect First Step Syndrome

Emergence rewards those who learn through doing, not those who plan through studying. The perfect first step never arrives because conditions change faster than plans perfect.

The Difference Between Testing and Exploring with Intent to Act

Kristian's story from Chapter 5 shows the power of exploratory action.

He invested less than a year exploring and acting: trying things, reflecting, and learning.

- Months 1–3: Didn't "research" entrepreneurship but launched a real online business with real customers.
- Months 4–6: Didn't observe health care but volunteered and worked full shifts in hospitals.

- Months 7–9: Didn't take coding classes but interned at a startup. At each phase Kristian demonstrated total commitment, asking for input from his mentors and listening to his intuition for inner clarity, not tentative piloting.

Leaders with an Industrial Age mindset ask "Should we?" People who are future-ready ask "Why not?" then proceed with "Let's try it!"

The distinction matters. Pilots create distance, with people in organizations testing ideas at arm's length, ready to abandon at the first difficulty. Commitment creates ownership, teams fighting to make things work because retreat isn't an option. The Meaning Cyclone demands this commitment. Customers sense authenticity. They know when organizations are testing versus committing. They respond to genuine belief, not tentative experiments.

Younger generations understand this intuitively. When they launch a business, they don't "test the waters." They dive in. Their TikTok isn't a pilot. It's their brand. Their side hustle isn't an experiment. It's their future.

Minimum Viable Product—Learning Through Doing

The antidote to going through the motions is not bigger bets or grander plans. It is smaller, fully committed experiments that generate real learning.

Minimum Viable Product (MVP)[7] is about learning faster. Future-ready navigators explore, then build the smallest, simplest version of a solution to test what they have discovered. That first MVP is not meant to be perfect. It is meant to be real, delivering just enough to generate honest customer feedback that shapes what comes next.

The concept is built into the core of Silicon Valley innovators but applies everywhere. An MVP is the smallest testable version of an idea that creates real learning. Not a prototype, not a pilot but a real product serving real customers, just with minimal features.

The 80 percent to 90 percent reality destroys perfectionist thinking. Most initial implementations won't work as originally conceived. That's not failure; it's data. The goal isn't getting it right first time. It's getting it right eventually through rapid iteration.

> This aligns perfectly with how Gen Zs approach careers. They don't expect to get it right first time, they expect to iterate rapidly. Job hop? They call it skill stacking. Side hustles? They call it portfolio careers. Failure? They call it content for their next LinkedIn post about lessons learned.

Real commitment shows up in calendars and budgets, not mission statements.

Small bets, big learning. That doesn't mean small commitment. It means full commitment to bounded experiments.

The difference matters. "Let's test this for six months and see what happens" is a pilot. It's polite paralysis. "Let's commit three weeks and $10,000 to solving this specific problem, and here's how we'll know it worked" is action. The commitment is total. The resources are real. The timeline is aggressive. But the blast radius is contained. You're not betting the company. You're betting enough to learn something useful, fast. Instead of analyzing what might work, you test what actually does work. Risk stops being something to avoid and becomes something to learn from.

Adobe Creative Cloud: Purpose, Exploration, Action

Here's what Adobe's transformation actually looked like—day to day, on the ground.

It wasn't "let's pilot a Creative Cloud solution." It was Narayen's unwavering commitment to becoming a service business—exploring and acting to deliver what customers actually need, not what internal roadmaps assumed they wanted.

It started with a deceptively simple question posed to customers, partners, and users: *"What do you need most right now?"*

Then we moved. Fast.

We created tiger teams that blended engineering with sales with marketing—people who had never collaborated before, suddenly shoulder-to-shoulder solving the same problem. They had days, not months, to build, refine, and deploy new approaches. Field teams worked around the clock—asking, testing, gaining commitment. Every week, all reconvened to share results with radical transparency: *"This worked. This didn't. That tanked—spectacularly."*

And then they went back out and did it again.

Act, ask, iterate. The cycle continued for months—not months of planning or piloting, but months of doing, learning, adjusting, and trying again.

Every few days, real insights surfaced: *"Photoshop users will pay $5 a month for continuous updates." "Illustrators want tablet integration." "Video editors are burning through more cloud storage than anyone projected."* The full picture didn't emerge from market analysis. It emerged from action and behavior—in real time.

By monitoring actual customer usage and delivering new capabilities based on what people were genuinely using most, solutions evolved one capability at a time. Instead of focus group feedback this was real bank card validation. Customers voted with their wallets, not their words.

The North Star was clear: loyal SaaS customers. With that purpose locked in, Adobe's tiger teams explored relentlessly—acting fast, evaluating usage, adjusting or scaling based on real data.

True commitment means being inflexible about the destination but completely flexible about the route.

A key factor in Adobe's successful transformation was the leadership team's willingness to let go of 25 years of assumptions, processes, business models, and ways of thinking. Letting go of yesterday's success requires courage—and belief in oneself and one's team to create what's needed today and into the future.

Leaders instinctively protect what made them successful, even when that protection guarantees failure. The same strategies that created past wins become barriers to future progress. Leaders defending today's revenue miss tomorrow's opportunity. But transformation has always started with someone choosing action over analysis—deciding that preserving the present matters less than creating what's next.

The Paradoxes That Drive Action

Industrial Age leaders worry: "If we move too fast, we'll sacrifice quality." The concern seems logical—careful work takes time, rushed work creates mistakes. But this assumption, like many Industrial Age beliefs, crumbles under examination.

Constraints accelerate action rather than limiting it. Unlimited resources create paralysis—too many options, too many debates. But give a tiger team three weeks and $10,000, and they'll solve problems that committees can't even define in six months. Boundaries don't limit action. Instead they focus it.

Commitment requires flexibility, not rigidity. Going all in doesn't mean rigid adherence to a plan. It means constant course correction toward a fixed destination.

Failure accelerates success instead of obliterating it. Organizations that fail fastest learn fastest. Each failed experiment eliminates wrong paths and uncovers right ones.

I don't care if you're not ready. No one's ready. The difference between people who succeed and those who don't? The successful ones move while the others prepare.

These paradoxes reveal a deeper truth about action in Emergence: the Industrial Age rules have reversed. What once seemed reckless is now essential. What once seemed prudent is now paralyzing.

McKinsey research makes the stakes clear. In a survey of more than 1,200 managers, only 20 percent of organizations excelled at making high-quality decisions quickly—yet those organizations were twice as likely to report financial returns of at least 20 percent from their most recent major decisions.[8]

The finding is unequivocal: faster decisions are not reckless decisions. They are better ones.

Now consider what's happening inside most organizations. Business leaders spend up to 70 percent of their time on decision-making. Yet fewer than half report that their decisions are timely. And 61 percent say at least half their decision-making time is simply wasted.

The problem isn't lack of information. It's lack of speed in making, then acting on the decisions.

Success Preservation

Adobe's transformation didn't begin with a new strategy. It began with a decision to let go of one. After 25 years of assumptions, processes, and a business model that had made the company wildly successful, the leadership team did something most organizations never dare: they released their grip on yesterday to create what was needed for tomorrow.

That takes courage. It requires confidence—in yourself and your team—that what you built before is proof you can build something great again.

Most leaders never get there. Instinct drives them to protect what worked, not realizing that protection has become the threat. The same strategies that created past wins now block future ones. Leaders defending today's revenue miss tomorrow's opportunity entirely.

Transformation always starts the same way—with someone choosing action over analysis, and deciding that preserving the present matters less than creating what's next.

The Empowerment Multiplier

Speed and quality improve when people closest to the work have authority to act. McKinsey research confirms what we've proven with clients: empowering those with direct customer contact creates 85 percent higher organizational decision quality.

At Adobe, transformation didn't happen through executive decisions. It happened through empowered action at every level. Account managers talking directly with customers. Product managers making feature decisions based on that input. Developers releasing updates based on real usage patterns. Our 40-person team didn't make those decisions. We empowered Adobe's people to act with speed, giving them authority within clear boundaries.

When decision authority goes to people with direct customer contact, the teams seeing problems firsthand, both speed and quality improve simultaneously. McKinsey found that empowered employees with sufficient coaching were 3.2 times more likely to make high quality and speedy decisions.

In emergence, those closest to the task at hand need authority to act. Bureaucracy disappears, learning accelerates, and quality improves through experience and feedback.

Tiger Teams: Structure for Speed

Efficient action by carefully structured tiger teams transform stalled initiatives into delivered results. Unlike Industrial Age committees, the tiger teams we use have distinct characteristics:

Size. 2–4 people maximum. Small enough for rapid consensus, large enough for diverse perspective across multiple areas of the business.

Timeline. 1–3 weeks. Long enough to generate real learning, short enough to maintain urgency.

Focus. One specific known problem. Not broad initiatives or vague objectives. Concrete challenge with measurable result.

Authority. Clear decision power within guidelines. Empowered to explore and act within agreed upon guidelines.

Resources. Real but bounded. Enough to test seriously, not enough to waste significantly.

Results. Success measured by specific metrics agreed in advance. Not activity reports, result measurements.

Our work with Barloworld, detailed later in this chapter, proved this at scale. Tiger Teams of three to four people accomplished in weeks what 18 months of planning couldn't.

Small actions with clear criteria beat big strategies with vague goals.

The difference is dramatic. Committees analyze what will be possible while tiger teams discover what actually works.

When to Stop Exploring and Start Acting

The shift from exploration to action isn't triggered by data completeness. It's triggered by recognition—an intuitive knowing with inner clarity—that learning through action will now exceed learning through analysis.

So how does one move forward?

It's simpler than you think. Pick one insight from exploration. One opportunity identified or possibility discovered. Just one.

Then pause, listen to intuition. Choose the direction based on inner clarity. Take that walk Shantanu Narayen took. Find that quiet space Marie created before her daily bike rides. Step away from the noise of external pressure and market panic. Give yourself the stillness to hear what you already know.

Then ask two questions: what is the most important action I can take right now to accelerate movement toward the North Star? And what will lead to real learning and results—not just motion?

Then trust what comes back. Trust your intuition. And move.

The knowing-doing gap kills more strategies than competition ever will.

Action begins with two brainwaves working in concert. Critical thinking evaluates the external: customer behavior, market realities, resource constraints, success metrics. Intuition reads the internal: your energy and your team's, the timing, the alignment with purpose. When both align—when analysis confirms feasibility and instinct confirms direction—stop deliberating. Commit.

Start small and specific. Choose one new tool or approach to use for three weeks. Define success measurements, timeline and resource requirements before beginning. If you can't describe what "working" looks like, you're not ready to act—you're ready to explore further.

The real challenge isn't finding the right opportunity. It's knowing when evaluation should continue versus becoming procrastination. Future-ready leaders feel that line. They balance analytical rigor with intuitive clarity, and they consistently outperform those who rely on either alone.

For leaders who want to move faster: stop asking employees to wait for approval. Give them a clear problem, defined boundaries, and success metrics—then get out of the way. They will deliver solutions through action while committees are still debating whether to act.

The shift from exploration to action begins with recognizing that you already have enough to start. Certainty doesn't precede action—it follows it. Learning happens through doing. Purpose gets closer through movement.

The Firefighter's Intuition

A client recently shared a story that perfectly captures importance of recognizing when to stop exploring and start acting. Her husband Steve, a retired firefighter with thirty years of experience, heard what sounded like an explosion. Massive smoke billowed from their neighbor's house.

Most people, including many trained firefighters, would sprint toward the door immediately. Industrial Age training says act fast in emergencies. But Steve did something different.

He moved slowly, deliberately, exploring the entire landscape. He scanned the property. He examined areas seemingly unrelated to the visible smoke. He didn't rush to action based on what was directly in front of him. He explored to determine what was ***really*** happening.

"Something felt different about this smoke," he explained later. "My training says do not rush. My gut said this was not a normal fire pattern. The smoke was too white, too concentrated. After thirty years, confidence in what I feel runs deeper than training."

His exploration revealed the truth: something stuck in the flue. No one in danger. Had he acted immediately on visible symptoms (smoke, explosion sound), he would have responded to the wrong problem.

Steve's approach shows the shift from exploration to action driven by intuition, not instinct from external pressure. He explored until his gut (his gut processing patterns faster than conscious thought) signalled: "This is different. Don't act on assumptions."

(*continued*)

(*continued*)

This is the timing emergence demands. Not rushing from exploration to action because it instinctively feels urgent. Not staying in exploration because uncertainty feels uncomfortable. Moving to action when internal knowing says "I understand what's actually happening."

Thirty years had trained Steve's nervous system to recognize patterns. His intuition knew when exploration was complete. That recognition, not a checklist or protocol, determined when to act, providing his neighbor with guidance on flue maintenance.

Why One Decision Changes Everything

While leaders at BlackBerry analyzed themselves into irrelevance, real change started with one future-ready person deciding to just do it—launch of the Handspring Treo.

Thousands of brilliant people at BlackBerry could have acted. Any engineer could build a touchscreen prototype in three months. Any product manager could launch an app store in six. Any executive could say "enough analyzing, ship something." No one did. No one had permission to challenge the sacred keyboard.

They built better keyboards while leaders at Apple built the future based on learnings from Handspring. Brilliant people, suffocated by Industrial Age permission culture, watching their company die in real-time while waiting for approval that never came.

Perfect plans executed too late lose to imperfect action taken now.

This principle of collective action through individual contribution appears everywhere transformation happens.

When the pandemic shut down live events overnight, wiping out his company's primary revenue stream, author Simon Sinek did not retreat into analysis or wait for perfect conditions. He asked every team member to generate 15 ideas within 48 hours.

"Not just one or two, but 15," Sinek has explained, "because the really good ideas wouldn't be the first or second but the 11th or 12th or 13th."[9] The exercise produced breakthrough ideas and created something more valuable: a culture of contribution rather than competition.

The constraint (15 ideas, 48 hours) became the catalyst. The urgency eliminated overthinking. The quantity requirement pushed past the obvious into the innovative.

The result was transformative—commercially and culturally. By pivoting to digital, Sinek expanded his reach far beyond what keynote touring allowed, growing his audience to more than 8 million followers and embedding his ideas on purpose-driven leadership into organizations across Europe, Asia, and Latin America. The Optimism Company shifted from revenue tied to individual speaking engagements to scalable, recurring income through online learning, subscriptions, and certified coaching programs. What the pandemic threatened to dismantle, the 15-ideas exercise helped rebuild—and multiply. The constraint didn't diminish Sinek's influence. It became the mechanism through which it compounded.

Action in Emergence demands purpose-driven grit: the determination to keep exploring, keep testing, keep learning even when results aren't immediate. The grit to fail fast, learn faster, and try again differently.

Action Delivers Results for Barloworld

Barloworld's transformation demonstrates what happens when you lead with Purpose—and what it costs when you don't.

They had spent 18 months on a digitalization strategy that was spinning its wheels. The reason? They'd started with technology instead of problems. This is classic Industrial Age thinking.

When I stepped in, the gap was immediately clear: no one had answered the most fundamental question—*why* digitalize? We reframed the entire initiative, ditching "Digitalization Strategy" in favor of a goal everyone could rally around: *improving operational efficiency and customer satisfaction to enable growth.* This wasn't just wordsmithing. It directly connected to Barloworld's corporate North Star—enabling progress in society—and to each team member's own objectives. Suddenly, the initiative had a heartbeat.

With Purpose established, Exploration moved fast. A tiger team of four—business leaders from two divisions, the treasurer, and IT—was chartered with a single mission: learn, sandbox, and critically evaluate AI tools to identify the best options for streamlining quarterly financial consolidation.

Three weeks later, they had a clear verdict: Microsoft Copilot ranked first, followed by Anthropic Claude.

Then it was time to Act. Each business leader formed their own tiger team—one division ran Copilot, the other used Claude. For three weeks, team leaders checked in regularly, exchanged real-time insights, and pushed each other. The result was decisive: while both tools delivered results, Microsoft Copilot met or exceeded every success criterion. The teams weren't just convinced—they were *confident*, ready to scale with Copilot.

We quickly moved into Collaboration mode. Learning labs created synergies as the shared learnings were captured to Empower others to deploy Copilot to consolidate financial reports from 15 subsidiaries across 25 countries—for board reporting.

What had once consumed days of painstaking administrative work would now be completed more efficiently and accurately, with AI flagging discrepancies that human eyes might miss. Most importantly, the team was liberated to do what only humans can do: analyze, interpret, and bring the story behind the numbers to the boardroom. This deeper analysis delivered real satisfaction internally and with the board members.

Eighteen months of stagnation. Twelve weeks to results. That's the power of P.E.A.C.E. in action.

When Action Is the Only Way Forward

Marie didn't pilot her bicycle ride through occupied territory. She committed. Every morning for three years, she explored the route and then acted. No perfect conditions. No permission. Purpose-driven determination that simply refuses to quit.

That's what Emergence requires. Not stubbornness but resolve. Not clinging to yesterday's route because it worked before, but navigating today's reality toward the same North Star.

BlackBerry clung to keyboards while the world moved to touchscreens. Kodak clung to film while photography went digital. The companies that thrive (Adobe, Apple, Netflix, Amazon) let go of what made them successful to build what was needed next.

Letting go is the hardest action Emergence demands. And it's non-negotiable.

Your Turn: Action Reflection

About current action:

- Where is hesitation disguised as strategy?
- What would "all in" look like for current organizational challenges?
- Which decisions need tiger teams instead of committees?
- What success metrics would measure progress toward the North Star?

About internal signals:

- How does intuition signal when to stop exploring and start acting?
- Where does fear of imperfection prevent learning through action?
- What energizes the team that strategy documents ignore?
- When did going internal last change a decision?

About real costs:

- What's the real cost of waiting versus the cost of acting?
- Where are pilots replacing real commitment?
- Which opportunities expired while analyzing?
- How much talent left during endless planning?

About generational knowledge:

- What would your most purpose-driven people do with the authority to act?
- Where is youthful impatience actually market timing?
- Which "reckless" ideas will be exactly right for Emergence?
- Who's already acting while others debate?

Action without purpose is just activity. Purpose without action is just philosophy. But even purposeful action has limits when attempted alone.

The next element of P.E.A.C.E. multiplies everything you've learned so far.

7 Collaboration: Moving from Consensus to Co-Creation

"If you want to go fast, go alone.
If you want to go far, go together."

—African proverb

In 1998, the business world celebrated what looked like perfect collaboration. Daimler-Benz merged with Chrysler Corporation in a $36 billion deal, creating one of the world's largest automakers.[1] Wall Street analysts called it brilliant. Business schools used it as a case study in global strategy: precision engineering meets entrepreneurial innovation. Together, they would dominate global automotive markets through complementary strengths. The press called it a "merger of equals." Executives promised unprecedented synergies.

Nine years later, Daimler sold 80 percent of Chrysler to private equity firm Cerberus Capital Management for $7.4 billion and even had to inject additional capital to sweeten the deal.[2] It was a collaboration failure. Two corporate cultures collided, and neither side would adapt. Both sides blamed the other. Meanwhile, tens of billions in value evaporated as integration plans failed to integrate anything.[3]

The operating models couldn't have been more different. Daimler embodied Industrial Age perfection: hierarchical decision-making, detailed protocols for every process, extensive documentation before action, quality standards considered non-negotiable. Chrysler operated using processes proven successful through emergence: flat organizational structures, collaborative teams, quick decisions made where problems emerged, informal communication across levels, innovation welcomed from anywhere.

The collision was immediate and brutal. Daimler executives expected detailed protocols. Chrysler teams expected brainstorming sessions. One side interpreted informality as unprofessional sloppiness. The other experienced formality as suffocating paralysis.

An executive later recounted a typical clash: a team member raised a concern in a meeting about a product decision. The response: "But we already agreed on this. Everything is detailed in the protocol." The reply: "What protocol? I saw documents but didn't consider them significant."

Neither approach was wrong. Without a common vision based on shared purpose, different approaches became destructive. Two world-class companies, operating in perfect silos, each convinced their way was the right way. Silos come from the belief that one approach is the only approach. Organizational chart boxes are the steps within the silo.

The DaimlerChrysler tragedy runs deeper than financial loss. Combined strengths could have created unprecedented automotive innovation. Precision engineering plus entrepreneurial speed should have been unstoppable. The missing element was clear shared purpose. And collaboration without shared purpose always fails. Neither company's leadership could answer the fundamental question: "Why does this combined entity exist?"

They had complementary capabilities but no aligned North Star.

Collaboration isn't everyone sitting in the room. It's engaging with the right people, aligned to the same why, working together so we move forward.

Confidence to Contribute

Collaboration only works when people confidently lean in, engage, and contribute openly. Google's Project Aristotle studied 180 teams and found what they called "psychological safety" was the single strongest predictor of team effectiveness. Not talent. Not resources. Not experience.

A feeling of safety that gives people the confidence to speak up, challenge ideas, admit mistakes, ask questions without fear. Without that, collaboration becomes a performance. People say what's safe, not what's true. Committees proliferate because they distribute compliments or blame. Tiger teams thrive because they distribute trust.

Why Committees Kill While Tiger Teams Thrive

The most expensive meeting? The one that ends without any decisions.

Every leader recognizes the pattern. Few have the courage to break it. "The stakeholder inclusion" trap requires every decision to pass through Legal, Procurement, HR, Compliance, Finance, and mysterious "key stakeholders" whose actual contribution remains unclear. By the time everyone's consulted, aligned, and documented, a three-person startup has already shipped, tested, and pivoted twice.

Leaders operating with Industrial Age mindset call this "best practice." They review and hire consultants to optimize meeting structures. They're perfecting the very process that's killing competitive advantage. They implement elaborate decision matrices, RACI charts defining who's Responsible, Accountable, Consulted, and Informed. They create steering committees to oversee working groups that coordinate task forces. Each layer adds delay without adding value.

War Rooms Outpace Conference Rooms

As described in Chapter 6, small tiger teams with a clear objective outperform elaborate structures. Adobe's transformation demonstrated this at scale. Engineering, sales, marketing, finance, and actual customers worked together intensively in war rooms. No PowerPoints. No departmental presentations. Just building together.

Hierarchy disappeared because only results mattered. Everyone contributed expertise while focused on the shared North Star: enabling creativity for all. They weren't evaluating from outside. They were immersed in creating together.

The difference is fundamental. Traditional conference rooms create distance. People presenting to each other, protecting territory, avoiding commitment. War rooms create immersion. People building together, sharing ownership, committed to results.

Tiger teams collaborate through clear purpose, short timeframes, and real challenges. Small size enables quick decisions. Bounded constraints create urgency. Most importantly, they aren't talking about a problem. They're immersed in it together.

"We Need to Roll Around in It"

In 2015, while leading change in Silicon Valley law firm Wilson Sonsini Goodrich & Rosati, I posed a simple question to a group of new recruits: "What's your preferred way of tackling a really complex problem?"

Their answer stopped me in my tracks: "We need to roll around in it."

No framework. No slides. Just immersion—getting deep into the problem together, exploring, experimenting, and learning until the path forward became clear enough to commit to.

It was one of the most honest and instinctively smart descriptions of effective problem-solving I'd ever heard. And it's exactly what the best tiger teams do—jump in head first, try things, and share learnings as they co-create solutions.

What Google Discovered That Most Leaders Ignore

Google spent two years and millions of dollars trying to answer one question: what separates high-performing teams from everyone else?

The results surprised them.[4] The best predictor of team effectiveness was not who was on the team. It was how they worked together. Google named it psychological safety: the shared belief that the team is safe for interpersonal risk-taking. Teams with high psychological safety shared specific behaviors. Members spoke in roughly equal amounts. They picked up on social cues, reading how teammates felt. They created space for everyone to contribute, including quieter voices. Most critically, they treated mistakes as learning opportunities rather than career threats.

> ***This connects directly to why tiger teams outperform committees. Tiger teams create psychological safety through bounded experiments with clear success criteria. Failure teaches rather than threatens. Committees create fear through undefined accountability and permanent judgment. Mistakes haunt rather than inform.***

Breaking Down Silos

In Chapter 4 we explored how purpose acts as the North Star. But organizations don't just have purpose—people do too. When individual purpose aligns with organizational purpose, you get $1 + 1 = 3$: a constellation of purpose. When it doesn't, you get friction, disengagement, and drag.

Cross-functional integration succeeds when people from different functions collaborate—bringing diverse experience and individual goals, yet moving toward a shared destination. Like stars in a constellation, they navigate from different positions, but they're all oriented to the North Star in the same sky. See Figure 4.1.

The Collaboration Evolution: From Consensus to Impact

People with an Industrial Age mindset call many things collaboration that simply aren't: committees seeking consensus, meetings avoiding decisions, stakeholder sessions protecting territory. Paperwork pretending to be teamwork.

The Industrial Age model worked—once. Involve all stakeholders. Document everything and ensure buy-in to minimize risk.

When building the Golden Gate Bridge or factories for car manufacturing, full alignment before action was important to prevent catastrophic failure. While it might have taken six-months, caution was the smartest strategy.

But today that model is now the enemy of progress.

Twelve-person alignment meetings where everyone talks, no one decides, and follow-up meetings get scheduled to discuss what was discussed. Marketing speaks about followers, engineering speaks specifications, sales speaks quota—and nothing moves. Three months later: beautiful process maps documenting how things should work, with nothing actually delivered.

The innovation workshop phenomenon of the early 2000s is the perfect case study. Two days of brainstorming. Hundreds of sticky notes and color-coded dots for voting. Elaborate action plans are created. The facilitator gets paid, the team feels productive—and absolutely nothing changes.

Meanwhile, a competitor's tiger team has already rolled out three MVPs with real customers. During Emergence, consensus-first collaboration doesn't reduce risk. It is the risk.

Silicon Valley: Speed Through Lean Teams

In Silicon Valley, we have a different approach to collaboration: it's all about speed through shared expertise. By gathering people who bring different perspectives, needs, and dreams together to explore, act, and share learnings, we co-create the future. Not committees but war rooms. Not consensus but rapid iteration.

Technology pioneers figured out what others haven't: collaboration without speed is elaborate procrastination. Everything happens through immediate action. When alignment appears in a coffee queue, action follows before the coffee cools.

From Tap on the Shoulder to Alliance by Friday

I'm standing in line at Peet's in Palo Alto. The person ahead is on a call about sustainable packaging for food delivery. I know someone building supply chain analytics for the food industry. I tap them on the shoulder: "Want a connection to a startup in analytics who's exploring food delivery?"

In most business cultures, this ends with polite interest: "Sure, what's their name," Maybe six months later, he sends a LinkedIn request. By then, the market has shifted twice.

> Before the coffee is ready, I've made the text introduction. That afternoon, they're on a call. By Friday, they're piloting an alliance. Purpose alignment in action. The developer is advancing his venture, so meeting an analytics expert passionate about his area becomes immediate priority. Only by understanding someone's purpose can collaboration happen.

Diversity enhances the process and outcome. Roughly 90 percent of Silicon Valley residents were born elsewhere, with nearly half from outside the United States. Everyone left something behind (family, familiar culture, comfort) running toward opportunity.

Collaboration is about building something outside of ourselves, gaining new knowledge, sharing, and ultimately survival.

Emergence: Purpose-Aligned Impact

Truly future-ready leaders recognize and leverage both approaches. They keep Industrial Age thoroughness where it matters: safety-critical decisions, regulatory compliance. They maintain Silicon Valley speed for market opportunities. They add something essential: purpose alignment that creates impact beyond individual capability.

Emergence collaboration happens when people share purpose. Collaboration that multiplies.

Young adults entering the workforce instinctively understand this evolution. They see collaboration as creating together: through Discord servers where programmers solve problems collectively, TikTok duets where creators build on each other's content, open-source projects where strangers contribute code. For them, collaboration is how creation happens.

Strawberry: Real Community Collaboration as Competitive Advantage When Petter Stordalen, founder of Nordic Choice hotel group, realized competing on hotel rooms was not sustainable, he transformed how his entire company collaborated with its partners, suppliers, and surrounding community.

Instead of viewing local businesses as competition for tourist dollars, leaders at Nordic Choice built partnerships with artists, restaurants, and cultural groups. Hotels became cultural connectors. Each property developed unique personality through local partnerships. Hotels transformed into community hubs where travelers and locals intersected, creating value none could generate alone.

The collaboration was genuinely symbiotic. Artists gained exposure to international audiences. Restaurants received qualified referrals from hotel concierges who knew their offerings intimately. Cultural groups found new audiences for their events. Guests experienced authentic local connection that no chain hotel could replicate.

Strategic collaboration that created competitive advantage through community connection.

Amazon and Whole Foods: Strategic Integration Amazon's acquisition of Whole Foods could have led to another culture clash disaster.

Tech giant swallows grocery chain, efficiency destroys quality, customers rebel. Instead, they demonstrated how purposeful collaboration between different organizational DNA can multiply value.

Amazon brought logistics mastery, technological infrastructure, and operational efficiency. Whole Foods contributed retail expertise, supplier relationships, and community connection. Success came from identifying intersection points where both purposes could flourish.

Instead of one culture absorbing another, they created spaces where Amazon's efficiency enhanced Whole Foods' quality, and Whole Foods' roots expanded Amazon's relationships and customer experience. Different approaches served a shared purpose of great customer experience and delivered results.

Adobe: Customers as Strategic Partners You've seen how Adobe's Creative Cloud transformation played out through action and exploration. Here is the collaboration secret that made it stick.

Adobe's collaboration extended beyond customers to suppliers and competitors. They open-sourced critical components, allowing smaller companies to build on their platform. They created partnerships with companies they'd previously sued for patent infringement.

The Meaning Cyclone had shifted their definition of success: from defeating competitors to expanding the creative ecosystem. Every tool built on their platform strengthened the whole offering. Every former competitor who became a collaborator multiplied Adobe's relevance.

ShoreTel: Collaboration Through Market Transformation In the mid-2010s, the communications market was shifting to cloud-based solutions. ShoreTel's strength (easy to use on-premise solutions) became a weakness. Next Step was engaged to accelerate their market transformation. In my work with the executive team, it was clear that they needed to rethink their market position, and go-to-market and delivery approaches.

The question was: "How do we maintain revenue growth in this changing market?"

We started with: what are you trying to achieve? The answer: growth through delivering brilliantly simple, unified communications solutions that are easy to use, reliable, and scalable.

That North Star clarity led to exploration: not in conference rooms but in the market itself. The real insight came from customers experiencing the shift, partners navigating the change, field teams watching competitors move daily.

Exploration revealed options: new alliances, different channels, fresh approaches to reaching customers, new pricing and delivery models.

Action meant fully committing to strategic shifts in how ShoreTel went to market. Not pilot programs. Genuine transformation requiring collaboration at every level. We worked with the executive team to refine the strategic direction, and with field managers to incentivize their teams to succeed and partnerships restructured.

Throughout, collaboration wasn't consensus-building or committee work. It was hands-on—executives, employees, customers, partners, and Next Step's team rolling around in it. By exploring, trying, acting, and sharing they shifted, exceeded revenue goals, and dominated a new market position. By working together, we created something no one could build alone.

Committees create consensus.
Collaboration creates results.

The result: ShoreTel's transformation led to a lucrative acquisition in September 2017. Mitel acquired ShoreTel for $430 million, immediately becoming the number two player in the global unified communication as a service (UCaaS) market. The combination nearly doubled Mitel's UCaaS revenue to $263 million. For ShoreTel's shareholders, the deal delivered a 28 percent premium over the prior closing price.[5]

> ***Collaboration serves a shared purpose: starting with clarity, exploring through market engagement, committing to bold action, empowering everyone to shape the result.***

Breaking the Boxes

The Industrial Age was built on boxes.

HR handles people, Engineering builds products, Sales talks to customers, Finance manages money. Each protects territory, optimizes metrics, defends budget. Collaboration happens through handoffs between boxes. Sequential, slow, political.

Emergence demands fluid ecosystems where boundaries dissolve based on need. Not organizational chaos. It's organizational evolution. Value flows to greatest impact rather than departmental ownership.

Gen Zs and truly future-ready leaders already operate this way. They don't identify as "marketers" or "engineers." They're creators, builders, problem-solvers. They learn whatever serves purpose, collaborate with whoever shares vision, reject job descriptions that constrain contribution. They build personal brands while working corporate jobs, launch ventures across industries, form partnerships that cross traditional boundaries.

Marie crushed the most dangerous boxes of all. At the German Air Force base, she served meals to soldiers who would have killed her if they knew what she was really doing. She hid food for Jewish prisoners. She listened to forbidden broadcasts. She helped refugees find safe passage. On the surface, she operated inside the box the occupation assigned her. Underneath, she collaborated across enemy lines with people she'd never met, serving a purpose none of them recognized.

Marie didn't collaborate across enemy lines because she read a book about breaking silos. She did it because the boxes could have killed her.

The walls between your teams aren't preventing life-threatening interactions. Which means you have even less excuse—and far more opportunity.

Adobe's transformation succeeded because they broke the boxes. Engineers worked directly with customers. Sales contributed to product development. Finance partnered on pricing. Everyone focused on enabling creativity rather than departmental metrics.

When engineering can't talk to customers because "that's sales' job," innovation dies. When great ideas filter through hierarchies, they arrive too late or too diluted.

Breaking boxes doesn't eliminate expertise.
It lets expertise flow where it's needed.

People contribute based on capability and passion, not title.

People thrive in emergence within ecosystems, not org charts. Collaboration happens wherever purpose demands it. Boxes become irrelevant when everyone navigates toward the same North Star.

Iceland Women's Strike

Ninety percent of Iceland's women stepped away from both paid work and unpaid care. Teachers, nurses, factory workers, mothers, bankers, cleaners. Different functions, different social positions, different daily realities. Aligned purpose: demonstrate women's indispensable contribution to society.[6]

No corporate hierarchy organized it. No government approved it. A group of women from across the political spectrum, liberals and conservatives, teachers and single mothers, formed a coalition. They called it a "day off" rather than a strike to protect participants from being fired under Iceland's labor laws. More than four months of organizing, they built coordination across every sector and every community. By October 24, 1975, the movement had reached national scale.

The country ground to a halt. No phones answered because operators were women. Newspapers did not print because typesetters were women. Flights were cancelled because flight attendants were women. Schools closed. Banks stayed open only because male managers agreed to work as tellers. No meals were cooked at home. Men brought children to work, and employers bought sweets and paper to keep them occupied. Iceland discovered what women's "invisible" work actually meant.

Different groups of women, working mothers, stay-at-home mothers, professionals, hourly workers, had different daily challenges. Their purposes aligned around one truth: women's work, both paid and unpaid, was essential and undervalued.

That single day of coordinated action reshaped Iceland's national identity. The next year, Iceland's parliament passed a law guaranteeing equal rights. Within five years, Vigdís Finnbogadóttir was elected president, the first woman in the world to be democratically elected head of state. She has said the 1975 strike paved the way. The collaboration of October 24, 1975, set Iceland on a path that has made it a global leader in gender equality for decades.

Fifty years later, when I met Iceland's President Halla Tómasdóttir,[7] she reminded me of this truth: transformation does not require organizational charts. It requires people with aligned purpose willing to collaborate across traditional boundaries.

Cross-functional integration in emergence. People from different positions, different functions, different daily realities collaborating because individual purposes align with shared destination.

Co-Opetition

Collaborating with competitors sounds contradictory. Industrial Age thinking says success comes from defeating rivals, protecting advantages, building moats. Emergence shows a different reality: some challenges are too big for any single organization to solve alone. Some opportunities multiply when suppliers collaborate on foundations while competing on applications. Co-opetition (simultaneous cooperation and competition) is strategic intelligence. It requires internal confidence: knowing purpose clearly enough that collaboration with competitors strengthens position.

Co-Opetition Through Internal Confidence

In Silicon Valley, Apple, Google, OpenAI, and Meta compete fiercely yet collaborate to address shared challenges. It is co-opetition, and it drives some of the fastest innovation on the planet.[8]

Co-opetition isn't based on company mission statements or years of trust. It stems from a common purpose: to build technology that has lasting impact on society.

Major tech companies contribute to the same Open Source technology base and leverage common data lakes. They collaborate on Linux kernel development and co-create web standards. Then they compete for customers based on unique offerings built from those same shared foundations.

While recognizing market competition, they align on the overall goal: bringing innovative technology to market. Their co-opetition works because they have clarity about their own differentiation ***and*** recognition that some problems are bigger than competition.

Cross-cultural collaboration amplifies the power of co-opetition. For decades, I have translated this concept and advised leaders to leverage the best of both "Silicon Valley Style" and "Traditional" mindsets.

Silicon Valley teams collaborate intensely while competing hard, sharing ideas, details, and solutions with confidence that their approach, product, differentiation will not be duplicated. After all, no one has time to re-create what someone else has built. European companies invest time building relationships and trust before sharing or collaborating.

Neither approach is wrong. Silicon Valley often wins on speed and volume while European companies create more sustainable long-term value.

The difference between strategic co-opetition and costly failure isn't the quality of the partners—it's the clarity of shared purpose.

I live this firsthand. As I bridge Silicon Valley and European business cultures, I empower innovators to appreciate European depth while encouraging European leaders to embrace Silicon Valley's speed and comfort with uncertainty. It's not about converting one mindset to the other. It combines the strengths of European leaders and Silicon Valley innovators into something neither could build alone.

That requires a rare leadership skill: the ability to recognize, appreciate, and bridge fundamentally different mindsets. To understand that collaboration doesn't look the same across geographies—and to draw out the best of each rather than forcing a single model everywhere.

This is where Industrial Age "scarcity thinking" breaks down. It says: "If they win, I lose." Emergence thinking says: "Real victories benefit everyone."

Today, the need for climate solutions, AI safety standards, and cybersecurity threat mitigation are simply too large, too complex, and too consequential for any single organization to solve. Leaders who have inner clarity on purpose recognize this. They stop fearing collaboration—and start recognizing when competing wastes resources better spent on co-creation of approaches to address shared challenges.

The Humanity Cyclone makes this evolution non-negotiable. As AI transforms every industry simultaneously, no single company can address all the implications alone. Those who collaborate on ethical AI standards while competing fiercely on applications will shape the future. Those who try to go it alone will be shaped by it.

Co-opetition is not compromise. It is strategy. But it only works when purpose aligns. Without that alignment, even the most promising collaborations become the most expensive mistakes.

Apple and Samsung: Co-Opetition in Action

Apple and Samsung demonstrate co-opetition at scale. They're fierce competitors in smartphones, tablets, and consumer electronics. Yet Samsung manufactures critical components for iPhone, including displays and processors worth billions annually.

It's strategic collaboration based on mutual benefit. Samsung gains guaranteed revenue and scale for its component business. Apple gets access to cutting-edge display technology and manufacturing capacity that would take years to build internally.

They compete viciously in retail stores while collaborating intensely in supply chains. They sue each other over patents while negotiating next year's component orders. This works because both have confidence in their own differentiation beyond shared components.

Apple knows Samsung's displays don't make Samsung's phones better than iPhones. Samsung knows supplying Apple doesn't weaken its own device business. Their purposes align on advancing technology while diverging on market positioning.

The Intelligence of Walking Away

Not all collaboration creates value. Some misaligned partnerships destroy it.

The hardest lesson about collaboration in Emergence: selecting partners carefully, knowing when to walk away and who to include. Industrial Age thinking says choose partners and include people based on status or title. Then gain consensus to ensure buy-in. But purposeful collaboration requires the discipline to choose carefully and invite only those whose purpose aligns with the North Star. Then say no when that alignment doesn't exist.

Energy vampires exist in every organization. They attend every meeting, contribute nothing, drain momentum. They ask for input then ignore it. They create elaborate processes that protect their position while preventing progress.

Recognizing these patterns isn't being "not nice," it's being strategic. Every hour spent in fake collaboration is an hour not spent on real value creation. Every meeting with misaligned partners delays progress toward the North Star.

Signs that collaboration will fail:

- No shared purpose despite repeated clarification attempts
- One party seeks consensus to avoid accountability
- Hidden agendas override stated objectives

Business models or personal goals are not aligned. Future-ready people who have adopted the emergence mindset instinctively recognize bad collaboration. They do not join committees for résumé building. They do not attend meetings without clear purpose. They leave organizations that waste their time with fake inclusion. Time and energy are finite resources. Previous generations learned this the hard way.

Sometimes the most collaborative act is working alone. When the vision is clear but explaining it would take longer than executing it. When the expertise required is so specialized that group input dilutes rather than enhances. When speed matters more than consensus.

Steve Jobs often worked from inner clarity. He knew when collaboration would enhance (Apple I) and when it would hinder (early iPhone development secrecy). The judgment to know which situation requires which approach: mastery.

Narayen did not collaborate on his decision to transform Adobe. He went for a walk alone, found clarity, then engaged others in execution. Collaboration on the vision would have diluted it. Collaboration on the implementation multiplied it.

Walking away from bad collaboration is intelligence. Purpose matters more than nice. Progress matters more than process. Impact matters more than inclusion.

With, Not For—The Next Step Way

Most consulting and service relationships run on the wrong model. Experts diagnose then consultants prescribe. Firms deliver complex reports for clients to implement or to call the consultants to come back and do it for them.

That creates dependency, not capability.

When I founded Next Step, I chose a different path—one built around my own Purpose: creating impact on society by empowering the leaders who shape it.

We start all engagements by going deep—understanding the client's purpose, the obstacles in the way, and what's actually needed to accelerate movement forward. Then I build a diverse team: people with hard-won experience in solving complex problems similar to what the client is facing.

What happens next is the real magic. Unlike traditional consulting firms, we don't research, create documents, or propose. We jump in, working alongside our clients—their people, their teams, their leaders—guiding navigation to their North Star. We co-create and guide implementation of the processes and teams that will carry them forward. We don't do it for them but with them.

Over weeks, months, sometimes years, we explore together, act together, and adapt together. The result isn't a deliverable. It's a future-ready organization with the capability—and the confidence—to keep *evolving long after we're gone.*

Don't catch the fish for people. Teach them to fish—then get out of the way.

The client picks up the fishing rod. My team's role is helping them cast, watching them land that first catch, stepping back as confidence builds. They develop pattern recognition. Their instincts learn to sense what's working before conscious analysis confirms it.

This approach frustrates leaders who want an expert to "just tell us what to do." It challenges the consulting model that maximizes billable hours through dependency. But it's the only approach that actually works to deliver lasting value.

You can't outsource navigation. You can't delegate confidence. You can't hire someone to follow your inner knowing for you.

But you can create the conditions where collaboration produces results nobody thought possible.

Global Collaboration Pays Off

Following Adobe's shift from software to services, digitalization and mobile apps exploded. Suddenly, one question dominated every boardroom: "How do we turn customers into loyal subscribers?"

While every company, industry, and region is unique, the core answer was surprisingly similar: get attention, make it easy to sign up, reward usage.

As word spread about my role in Adobe's, Autodesk's, and Microsoft's transformations, my inbox overflowed. I got emails from Avinor, Posten, Schneider Electric, TechnipFMC, and RaboBank. Different industries. Different countries. Same need: digitalize or fall behind.

I saw an opportunity. By bringing these leaders together—across industries, backgrounds, and borders—and facilitating their learning in focused Executive Growth Circles, I could have real impact. Not as their consultant. As their catalyst.

The Executive Growth Alliance is P.E.A.C.E. in action (see Figure 7.1). Leaders join with **Purpose**. Through facilitated discussions they **Explore** possibilities and alternatives to a common challenge. All leave each circle committed to **Action**. Between circles they **Collaborate**, testing new approaches in the real world. Through shared learning, all are **Empowered** to strengthen their organization's future-readiness.

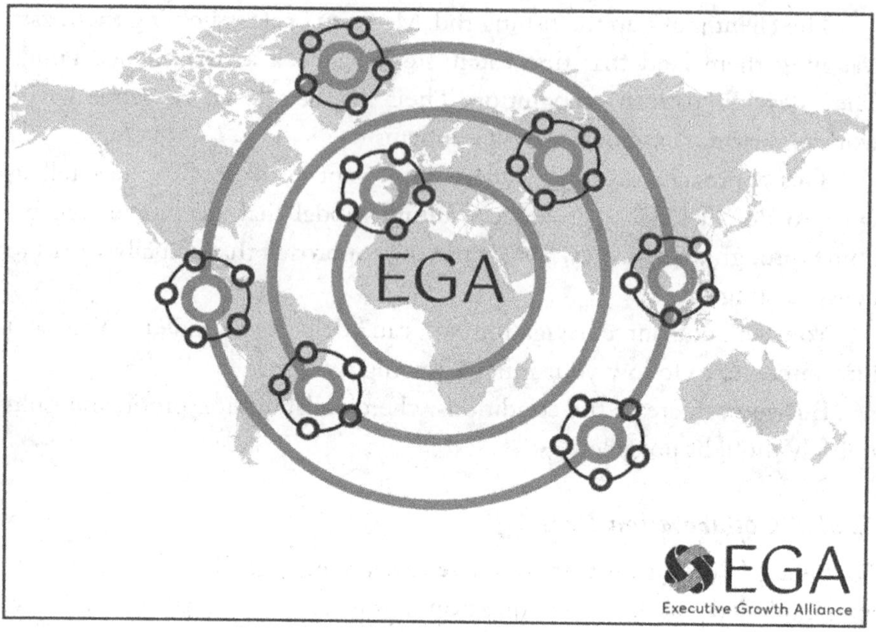

Figure 7.1 Executive Growth Alliance.

Outside the Box, Inside Nine Months

In 2018, leaders from Avinor (Norwegian Airport Authority) and Posten (Norwegian Post) left an Executive Growth Circle committed to taking action. Within nine months, they and volunteers from their companies had taken an idea from concept through development to a live test with real customers at Oslo Airport—checking baggage delivered by Posten via the MyBag app.

Two public sector organizations. Different mandates, different cultures, different bureaucracies. Collaboration outside the boxes paid off.

Purpose-driven. Cross-boundary. Focused on outcomes, not process.

Future-readiness doesn't come from an expert, a book, or a research project. It comes through experience—exploring, trying, learning, adapting.

As Emergence accelerates and traditional walls crumble, dependency on consultants and legacy reputation becomes fatal. The leaders who thrive will be the ones collaborating with others as they navigate toward their North Star, building the capability to succeed whatever comes next.

Why Collaboration Isn't Optional

The numbers prove what Silicon Valley practices daily: collaboration is not nice-to-have team building. It is the strategic multiplier that separates survival from thriving.

Diverse teams make better decisions up to 87 percent of the time compared to individuals, with the advantage increasing as teams add diversity in gender, age, and geography.[9] Companies with executive teams in the top quartile for ethnic and cultural diversity are 36 percent more likely to outperform their peers on profitability.[10] Organizations that promote collaborative working are five times more likely to be high-performing.[11]

But here is the statistic that should concern every leader: 64 percent of workers report losing at least three to five hours of productivity per week because of poor collaboration.[12] More than a third of a working day, wasted because people cannot work together effectively.

These are not soft metrics. They are hard financial reality. The Speed Cyclone punishes slow decision-making. The Confidence Cyclone rewards consistent delivery. The Meaning Cyclone demands purposeful contribution. Organizations that cannot collaborate effectively fail on all three.

The Collaboration Paradoxes

Real collaboration doesn't happen in conference rooms. It happens when purpose-aligned people create together what none could achieve alone.

During emergence, collaboration becomes more critical. It evolves in ways that people using an Industrial Age mindset can't comprehend:

- **Less is more.** A three-person tiger team outperforms a twelve-person committee. Barloworld's tiger team achieved more in two months than committees had in eighteen. The Speed Cyclone rewards small teams that move fast over large groups that move carefully.

- **Competition enables cooperation.** Google, Microsoft, and Amazon (fierce competitors) collaborate on Linux development and share data lakes. Internal confidence about their own differentiation enables external collaboration. The strongest competitors make the best collaborators when purpose aligns.
- **Individual confidence enables collective success.** When people have confidence in their own judgment, they can genuinely value others' contributions. Internal confidence eliminates ego protection and territorial behavior.
- **Walking away enables coming together.** Sometimes the most collaborative act is working alone. Steve Jobs worked alone on vision, then collaborated intensively on execution.

These paradoxes reveal why DaimlerChrysler failed. They had everything traditional collaboration required. They lacked what emergence demands: shared purpose that transcends difference.

P.E.A.C.E. in Action

P.E.A.C.E. occurs dynamically not as a sequence. DaimlerChrysler tried sequential collaboration: first merge, then align, then integrate. Adobe's leaders continually evaluated purpose, explored broadly, acted quickly, collaborated openly, and empowered customers to create in new ways.

Future-ready leaders who are thriving with emergence don't move through P.E.A.C.E. like a checklist. They live it.

Your Turn: Collaboration Reflection

Most teams call it collaboration. It's often something else.

The honest assessment:

- Where does control block collaboration?
- What structures reinforce silos rather than connection?
- Which decisions need tiger teams instead of committees?
- Where does fake collaboration mask real dysfunction?

About internal dynamics:

- How can individual internal confidence accelerate team momentum?
- Who feels unheard or underutilized?
- What would change if every voice had equal weight?
- When did going internal last change team direction?

About strategic possibilities:

- Where does lack of purpose alignment prevent real collaboration?
- How will co-opetition solve shared challenges?
- What complementary strengths could multiply impact if combined?
- Which energy vampires need to be excluded?

About generational knowledge:

- What would young professionals build if given collaborative authority?
- Where is "process" blocking progress?
- How will Discord-style collaboration replace conference rooms?
- Who's creating while others are meeting?

Collaboration without purpose is just expensive meetings. Purpose without collaboration limits impact. But even the best collaboration has a ceiling without the final element of P.E.A.C.E.

Steve, the firefighter had internal confidence to assess the situation. He had the expertise to collaborate if needed. But what made him truly effective was having the authority to act on his judgment, the empowerment to make decisions without seeking permission.

DaimlerChrysler had talented people on both sides who could collaborate brilliantly. They didn't. Hierarchical structures strangled empowerment. Decisions required approval through layers. Innovation died in committee review. The best ideas never reached implementation because the people who had them lacked authority to act. Meanwhile, Toyota was empowering line workers to stop production immediately to fix problems. One company trusted people closest to the work. The other trusted hierarchy. The results showed in market share.

Collaboration built the bridge. Empowerment decides who gets to cross it.

8 Empowerment: Releasing Power That Already Exists

> "The best executive is the one who has sense enough to pick good men to do what he wants done, and self-restraint enough to keep from meddling with them while they do it."
>
> —Theodore Roosevelt

Ritz-Carlton famously empowers every employee, from housekeeping to management, to spend up to $2,000 per guest to solve problems or create memorable moments, per incident, without approval or escalation.[1]

The philosophy is revolutionary: trust people to make judgment calls that traditionally require management approval. If a guest mentions concern about missing their daughter's graduation due to flight delays, the concierge can arrange a helicopter lift to the site. If an anniversary dinner reservation gets lost, a waiter can create an entirely personalized experience that exceeds the original plan. The housekeeper who notices a guest struggling with mobility can immediately arrange upgraded accessibility features. All without asking anyone.

Meanwhile, Fortune 500 executives still trapped in Industrial Age thinking need three signatures for a $500 purchase. Middle managers can't change a process without committee approval. "Empowered" team leads can't hire, fire, or adjust a deadline without escalating. Companies with billion-dollar budgets require procurement reviews for software subscriptions that cost less than a week's worth of coffee.

First there are Conference rooms named "Innovation Hub." Then there are leadership workshops called "Unleashing Potential." There are also motivational posters of mountain climbers under words like "Ownership" and "Autonomy."

Then reality: teams spending more time seeking permission than solving problems.

Ritz-Carlton's philosophy: "Ladies and gentlemen serving ladies and gentlemen." When people see themselves as ladies and gentlemen, they act differently than when they see themselves as employees. The $2,000 sends a message: "We trust your judgment." That confidence transforms service from transaction into relationship.

The Confidence Cyclone rewards this approach. Customers trust people empowered to solve problems, not policies. The Speed Cyclone demands it. While competitors escalate through approval chains, Ritz-Carlton's people solve problems immediately.

Yet most organizations do the opposite. They create elaborate empowerment programs while maintaining every structure that prevents power from emerging. They talk about empowerment while desperately maintaining control.

Right now, as the cyclones collide and markets shift daily, empowerment isn't optional. It's survival.

Letting go of control is the hardest leadership challenge.

Empowerment is not permission.
It's a clear perimeter and the trust to move inside it.

The Trust Gap

Empowerment scares leaders because it asks them to do the hardest thing: let go.

Let go of controlling every step. Let go of the comfort that comes from approving every decision.

Leaders announce empowerment while gripping control with both hands. The words say "I trust you." The behavior says "but check with me first."

The pattern breaks when the leader has the inner confidence they can recover, adapt or pivot to a new approach when something goes wrong.

The Perimeter Is the Point

This is precisely why empowerment fails in most organizations. It isn't too much freedom. It's the wrong kind. Handing someone a laptop with vague objectives and saying "check in next week" isn't freedom. It's abandonment with a deadline.

Navigators who get this right don't question what they empower people to do—they define the perimeter and what exists inside it.

When Netflix tells employees to "act in Netflix's best interest," that phrase carries enormous context: deeply communicated values, explicit business priorities, and a culture that clearly communicates what "best interest" actually means in practice. The boundary is invisible but real. When Ritz-Carlton gives every employee—from housekeeper to concierge—the authority to spend up to $2,000 per guest to solve a problem without approval, the boundary is precise: guest experience, in this moment, without escalation. Not unlimited authority. Purposeful authority.

When Shantanu Narayen told Adobe's executive team "I don't have the answers—I have a team of bright people who need to go figure it out in the next month," he wasn't abdicating. He was setting the clearest possible perimeter: the purpose was democratizing creativity, the timeline was urgent, and the team had complete freedom to navigate toward the North Star. The structure didn't constrain empowerment. It created the conditions for it.

Without that structure, empowerment becomes abandonment. With too much of it, empowerment becomes micromanagement wearing a different mask. The breakthrough happens when boundaries are clear enough to create confidence yet loose enough to enable creativity.

Constraints don't limit empowerment. They enable it.

The Playground Principle

Leaders with an Industrial Age mindset get empowerment backwards. They think it means removing guidance or boundaries and letting people "figure it out." That's not empowerment. That's abandonment.

Take a six-year-old to Central Park's 843 acres and say "Go play. I'll be back in an hour." That's insane. But it's exactly how most companies "empower" people. They hand someone a laptop with vague objectives and say "check in next week and let me know what you have sold, created, delivered."

Now take that same child to a playground with perimeter fencing, age-appropriate equipment, and clear sight lines. Say: "I'm going to get a coffee and be back in 15 minutes. When I return, I want to see how great you are at swinging and going down the slide. Stay inside the fence."

From Permission to Perimeter

In the Industrial Age, empowerment was a nicety granted by a boss. When you were rewarded with a certain title such as director, you were ushered into a narrow box. Step outside that box, ask for permission. A system built on fences that kept people small and safe.

Then came the Agile era, which promised to flatten everything. Offices and titles disappeared, replaced by something just as exhausting: the illusion of flatness. Without clear structures, "empowerment" became a game of social capital. Who you knew. How loud you could shout in a Slack channel. Not true empowerment. Just a different kind of noise.

In Emergence, empowerment is about clarity of the perimeter and the reason it exists.

This is what Novartis understood when CEO Vas Narasimhan launched the "Unbossed" initiative.[2] The name itself was the message: stop waiting for the boss to tell you what to do. But Unbossed didn't mean unstructured. Leaders defined a massive, clear perimeter based on one thing: Patient Impact. Once that fence was visible, people stopped huddling in the middle waiting for instructions. They started running to the edges.

The shift: stop trying to "empower" people by giving them permission to act within a "span of control." Instead, build a Purpose Perimeter so strong and so clear that people don't feel the need to ask for permission at all. If it's inside the fence of the shared purpose, the answer is already "Yes."

This demands letting go at every level. Leaders let go of approving individual decisions. Managers let go of dictating methods. Teams let go of waiting for direction. The perimeter holds everyone accountable without anyone holding the reins.

Purpose Alignment: The Empowerment Accelerator The single most powerful way to amplify empowerment isn't better training, clearer processes, or fancier tools. It comes from aligning a person's individual purpose with the organization's North Star. When that alignment exists, empowerment stops being something granted and becomes something that simply exists. The leader's job shifts from "empowering people" to removing obstacles so people can accelerate achievement of purpose.

The Empowerment Paradoxes

Empowerment during Emergence operates through paradoxes that Industrial Age thinking can't process.

- **Letting go creates alignment.** The tighter leaders grip control, the more dysfunction emerges. People outsmart approval systems. Talented individuals leave. Innovation dies in committee review. When people have clear purpose and real authority, alignment happens naturally. Leaders at Ritz-Carlton set the purpose, not the decisions. The result: thousands of employees making aligned decisions without oversight. Consistency through letting go.
- **Confidence matters more than competence.** Competence is knowing how to do something. Confidence is knowing you can succeed—sometimes by figuring it out. Empowerment grows from confidence because confident people learn what they do not know, while competent people without confidence never try to learn. Real empowerment builds internal capacity to navigate without external direction. Owned capability that travels with the person.
- **Walking away enables staying.** Workers aged 25–34 have a median tenure of just 2.7 years.[3] People early in their careers move when they cannot make meaningful impact. Leaders who empower people to leave paradoxically inspire them to stay. When people know they can go, they choose to remain. When people feel trapped, they plan their exit. Letting go of retention control creates retention.

These paradoxes reveal why traditional empowerment programs fail. Leaders try to teach empowerment while maintaining control structures. They preach autonomy while requiring approval. They celebrate ownership while hoarding authority. Every paradox demands the same thing: letting go of the old model to allow the new one to emerge.

Capability First

Empowerment without capability or confidence is a recipe for failure. Handing someone authority they're not ready to take on doesn't develop them. It can destroy the confidence they do have.

The key to successful empowerment is building capability and releasing authority at the same time. As the employee's confidence grows, so do the results.

Real Empowerment in Practice: Adobe's Evolution

For me, the most powerful moment in Adobe's transformation wasn't a strategy deck or a product launch. It was one sentence: I don't know.

When Narayen announced the decision to shift from selling software to becoming a digital experience company, his executive team responded with a typical question: ***How*** are we going to do that?

Questions at him from all directions. How are we going to price it? How will delivery work? What about our partners? How do we handle sales compensation?

Narayen's answer: "I haven't a clue. I don't have the answers."

Then he looked around the table at 12 senior leaders and said something that changed everything: "But what I do have is 12 people around this table who are bright, successful, determined, and committed. If you're not committed, get out now. Those who are committed, I'm empowering you to work with your teams of equally bright people and figure it out. Time is ticking. Go start collaborating with your teams, customers, partners to explore potential answers to the questions you are asking."

That moment is what this chapter is about. Narayen let go of needing to have the answers. He let go of controlling the method. He let go of the Industrial Age expectation that the person at the top provides the plan and everyone else executes. What he held onto was purpose: in five years, Adobe would no longer be a software company. Everything else was for his empowered teams to figure out.

What matters here is that moment of letting go. One leader chose to hold onto purpose and release everything else. And thousands of people rose to fill the space he created.

Technology Frees People for What Matters

In the early 2010s, grocery store managers everywhere faced the same problem—attracting and retaining young cashiers. Scanning barcodes and weighing produce for hours is simply not exciting work.

A regional chain in central Europe found what sounded like the perfect solution: self-checkout. Lower costs, less employee friction.

Reality surprised them. Customers avoided the empty self-service stations, choosing instead to wait in long lines for the remaining human cashiers. I received a call from the frustrated CEO. "I understand your company drives change. Come down here and figure out why people aren't using the self-checkout."

When I arrived, I started where I always start: "Tell me what you really want to achieve."

The answer: "More profits and increased customer loyalty. With less hassle."

We talked with the customers standing in line. The quick answer was that they didn't feel confident using the new machines. So, the manager assigned someone to guide customers through the process.

It worked. Briefly. Yet, even after learning the system, people reverted to the human checkout line.

Then we discovered the real issue. The majority of customers didn't want faster transactions. They wanted human connection. Yet, the manager had already invested in the machines.

My suggestion: what if we provided the cashiers with key food and nutrition information and empowered them to develop expertise in meal prep, produce, meat etc. to help customers make broader choices.

One cashier became a produce specialist, discussing seasonal vegetable pairings. Another specialized in meat, advising on cooking methods. A third focused on dairy, offering recipe suggestions. Barcodes were scanned by machines. Relationships were built by people.

Within six months: profitability increased 150 percent. Customer loyalty tripled. Employee satisfaction soared as work aligned with individual interests and strengths.

Technology freed people from what they hated (scanning barcodes) and developed them into what customers actually valued.

Today, AI is freeing people everywhere.

What might your company become with people amplified by AI?

The leaders who are winning right now all follow the same pattern: "let go of controlling how work gets done, use technology to handle what drains people, and empower people to contribute where their human capability creates real value."

The leader's job isn't to manage the technology or manage the people. It's to create the conditions where both can do what they do best.

By setting up sandboxes in which navigators can explore, act, roll around in new approaches—leveraging people and technology, future-ready leaders achieve real measurable results.

It's not through open-ended experiments with no boundaries—there are clear perimeters, real business challenges and freedom inside the perimeters to explore, test, and build.

Barloworld's tiger teams proved this in practice. Four to eight weeks. Specific budgets. Clear success criteria. Within those guardrails, teams chose their own tools and approaches—including AI tools most had never touched before. Nobody waited for permission or a training program.

The constraints didn't limit innovation. They ignited it.

Tito Guerrero: When Empowerment Changes Everything About 12 years ago, my company Next Step was engaged by Goodwill International where I met Tito Guerrero.

Tito was one of the most driven, effective, lean-in people in the Goodwill Greater East Bay organization. As director of operations, he was constantly seeking ways to learn, grow, and make things happen—not just for the organization, but for everyone around him.

After we'd worked together for a couple of years, he asked me to lunch. He wanted a sounding board. Then he told me his story.

In his early twenties, Tito made a mistake that changed everything. In his words, he "killed his best friend." He went to prison for more than a decade.

While incarcerated, he made a commitment: to spend the rest of his life paying back what could never truly be repaid. He worked relentlessly—completing every education program available, taking every prison job offered, doing everything possible to be primed for success after release.

While Tito submitted more than 500 applications and went for many interviews for work as an optician, for which he had gained certification during his time in prison, Goodwill Greater East Bay expanded their post-incarceration program.

> ***Goodwill's purpose: empowering and creating opportunities for disadvantaged people—those coming out of hospitals, mental institutions, or prisons. They do this through collecting donations that are then sorted, cleaned, priced and delivered to retail locations from which they are sold—all by team members selected, trained and developed to succeed in the workplace.***

Tito joined as an intern. He worked with an intensity that surprised no one who knew his story. When he was released from prison, Goodwill hired him as a driver.

Within a few years, Tito was promoted to director of operations. Then vice president. He earned his bachelor's degree. Then his MBA.

Over lunch that day, he shared the realization that had been shaping every decision since prison: his purpose in life is to make a difference for others. To give back. To help people accept themselves, love others, and think carefully about each action they take.

Since then, Tito has empowered thousands—as Senior VP of Operations, as a speaker, and as a coach to people in local prisons, young people at risk, and those who have given up on themselves. He gives people a sense of hope when every system around them says they're beyond it.

Real empowerment isn't a program or a policy. It's genuine belief in what someone can become.

Tito's story illuminates what Chapter 1 revealed about mismatches: when people are measured by past mistakes rather than future potential, the exact capabilities Emergence demands get wasted. Grit and purpose and the determination to navigate through the cyclones lead to meaning through the hardest circumstances.

Novartis: Empowerment Through Structural Fluidity

Most organizations treat structure as reality—org charts carved in stone, job descriptions that outlast the problems they were designed to solve. Novartis made a different choice. Leadership redesigned the entire operating model around a single North Star: improving patient lives. And then they did something most leaders find nearly impossible. They let go.

Rather than assigning work based on titles and reporting lines, Novartis matches people to the problems they care about most deeply. If an employee believes they would be more valuable in immunology than neuroscience, they move.

Team members participate in dynamically designing structure that serves the purpose. The result is an organization that reorganizes itself every four to seven months, not in crisis, but in response to where the work is and which people are best equipped to do it.

This is empowerment as architecture, not authority.

The Novartis Innovation Sandbox takes it further. Each team enters with two things clearly defined: the purpose they are serving and the boundaries within which they operate. Inside that perimeter, everything else is open. No prescribed methodology. No predetermined solution. Teams create, test, iterate, and build—fully accountable to the outcome, fully free in how they pursue it. The boundary is not a constraint. It is the condition that makes genuine freedom possible. Without it, exploration becomes chaos. With it, exploration becomes innovation.

> This is the pattern Emergence demands of leaders: state the purpose, define the boundary, then step back. Empowered, purpose-aligned people don't need managing. They need room.

The Most Dangerous Organizational Disease

The most dangerous addiction today isn't to substances. It's the need to control everything.

I don't care how many empowerment workshops you've attended. If people still need permission to make decisions, you haven't empowered anyone. You've just talked about it.

This obsession destroys potential everywhere—in companies, families, schools, communities. Twelve-person councils spend weeks gaining consensus before three people can test a solution. Organizations spend six months teaching delegation, then require approval for every meaningful decision. The bottlenecks move slower than the problems they're designed to solve.

While you're scheduling alignment sessions, competitors are solving customer problems in real time.

The personal cost compounds fast. Talented people leave. Others learn helplessness instead of capability. Communities stagnate. All because someone couldn't let go.

Control addiction comes from fear—fear that without constant oversight, everything falls apart. As Chapter 2 revealed, this fear is biological. The amygdala fires faster than conscious thought when facing uncertainty. The substantia nigra craves familiar patterns, rewarding control over risk.

But Emergence reveals the opposite. When people have clear purpose and internal confidence, control becomes unnecessary. Alignment happens naturally. Results improve. Innovation accelerates.

The antidote isn't another delegation workshop. It's the internal confidence that lets leaders release control and trust purpose-aligned people to act. When leaders trust their own judgment, they don't need to control others' decisions. When people believe in their capability, they prove it.

A sandbox with clear borders gives people space to play, try, and act. However, if the people inside it are still looking around for permission, nothing really happens. True empowerment happens when people have real ownership. Future-ready leaders must let go of the need to control what happens in the sandbox.

Your AI Prompt Is a Leadership Test Those anchored in an Industrial Age mindset treat AI like a search engine—or worse, an assistant they can bark orders at: "Give me two companies doing customer retention well." They assign tasks. They expect specific deliverables. They get frustrated when AI gets it "wrong." They want someone else to do the work—even when that someone is software.

Future-ready navigators approach AI as a thinking partner: "Our enterprise division has seen a 15 percent decline in customer retention over two quarters. Our growth plans depend on expanding B2B customers' use of our platform, so we need to address this now. What might we be missing?"

Notice the difference. The first demands an answer. The second invites insight.

And the future-ready navigator doesn't stop there. They go deeper: "How are other companies in our sector addressing retention right now?" Or: "Based on our analytics, what do you see as our most critical blind spots affecting customer loyalty?"

This is the shift. AI is a tool, a thinking partner, another set of eyes—not a servant hired to produce deliverables. It thrives on context, nuance, and the quality of questions you bring to it.

Here's what I find fascinating: the leaders who are best at leveraging AI are the same ones who truly empower people. That's not a coincidence. Both require the same skill—using context, asking better questions, and getting real valuable input.

The concern I hear most from leaders is AI safety. "How can we reduce the risks of unleashing AI? How do we protect our data?"

The answer is building in guardrails that enable, not restrict use. First commit to a corporate license and ensure the company-wide AI policy stipulates which tools are licensed for use. Build your own company LLM to ensure sensitive data remains in an enclosed area. Then empower people to use the approved tools fully. Not "be careful using AI." Instead: "Here are the tools. Here are the boundaries. Now go."

This is the playground principle applied to technology. The fence isn't there to limit play. It's there to make play safe enough to be bold.

As AI handles routine work, human value shifts to judgment, creativity, connection. People in organizations that empower their teams to use AI tools to amplify their own capabilities and free them to deliver greater value outperform those still trying to control both humans and machines.

The $75 Million Contrast

Empowerment doesn't always work. Sometimes it creates chaos instead of capability. The warning signs of fake empowerment:

- Authority without accountability—do whatever, no consequences
- Responsibility without resources—own this, but no budget
- Freedom without frameworks—figure it out, no boundaries
- Delegation without development—handle this, no support

Sometimes empowerment fails because people aren't ready. Not everyone has developed the judgment—or shares enough purpose—to align naturally.

That doesn't mean reverting to control. It means building trust progressively: small authorities, clear wins, expanding freedom alongside growing capability.

But here's the truth: most empowerment doesn't fail because of too much freedom. It fails because organizations spend millions teaching empowerment while keeping every control structure that prevents it.

$75 Million to Laminate a Permission Slip

One composite example—"InduManufacturing Corp"—represents a pattern I've seen repeatedly across industries and continents. An industrial systems manufacturer commits $75 million and 18 months to a comprehensive empowerment initiative. They hire two consulting firms to conduct assessments.

(*continued*)

(continued)

Nine hundred employees complete "delegation inventories"—carefully documenting the decisions they wish they were allowed to make. An elaborate governance framework arrives, 100-plus checkpoints strong, color-coded and laminated. "Empowerment Champions" are appointed in every department, armed with slide decks and enthusiasm, tasked with evangelizing the "new culture." Town halls are held. Values are reposted on walls. Leadership celebrates the initiative in the annual report.

The result? Employees still needed three signatures for a $500 purchase. Same approval processes. Same bottlenecks. Same talent exodus to scaleups in which they can build, deploy, promote on day one.

The pattern repeats because leaders with an Industrial Age mindset try to implement empowerment rather than release it.

Meanwhile, companies that actually empower don't workshop it—they practice it. People in Novartis aren't taught to reshape structure. They have authority to do it. Adobe doesn't teach customer collaboration. They live it. Ritz-Carlton doesn't teach trust. They demonstrate it through discretionary authority.

Navigators recognize purpose matters more than pay. They don't want empowerment workshops—they demand actual empowerment. They recognize that technology and customer needs will continually reshape their jobs. They're adapting. The question is whether their organizations will keep up.

How to Empower Without Abdicating

Empowerment isn't abdication. Leaders don't hand over responsibilities and hope for the best. They shift from controlling work to enabling workers, from making all decisions to ensuring the right decisions get made by the right people.

- **Set the North Star, not the route.** Leadership means pointing toward the North Star, not providing GPS coordinates for every turn. When Netflix decided to become a streaming company, Hastings didn't dictate how every team should execute. He set direction. Then teams figured out content strategy, technology infrastructure, and user experience on their own terms. The route changed constantly. The North Star never wavered.

- **Create guardrails, not gates.** Guardrails provide boundaries within which people move freely. Amazon's "two-way door" decision framework is a good example: reversible decisions can be made quickly by anyone, while irreversible decisions require more deliberation. One simple rule creating massive empowerment. Instead of approving every expense, set spending authorities. Instead of reviewing every communication, establish brand guidelines. Instead of signing off on every hire, define competency standards.
- **Recognize humanity, not only results.** Most leaders celebrate results: revenue generated, projects completed, problems solved. To build real empowerment, celebrate the behaviors that create those results: smart risks taken, decisions made without escalation, problems solved before becoming crises. When leaders recognize independent decision-making, it encourages more. When they celebrate cross-functional collaboration happening without management involvement, it reinforces the behavior.

Empowerment That Multiplies Beyond You

The ultimate test of empowerment: does it survive your absence? Marie didn't issue commands at the bridge. She created shared purpose. People who had never led found themselves guiding others to safety. Those she empowered began empowering others. Families she saved went on to save others. This is empowerment's true measure. Not what happens in your presence, but what continues in your absence.

Your Turn: Empowerment Reflection

One question first: if leadership disappeared for two weeks, would progress stop or accelerate?

Where control lives:

- Where are decision-making bottlenecks in the organization?
- Who's waiting for permission to do work they're already capable of?
- What decisions get made by people furthest from the problem?

About readiness:

- Who's ready to lead if control was released?
- What's one decision that could be delegated for 30 days?
- Which control mechanism gets removed this week?

About internal dynamics:

- Are you building problem-solvers or creating dependency?
- What happens when people act on purpose instead of permission?
- How does going internal guide your empowerment decisions?
- Where does fear masquerade as prudent oversight?

About generational knowledge:

- What would your navigators build with real authority?
- Where is "process" preventing progress?
- Who's creating while others are controlling?

Empowerment is about being effective. In markets moving at digital speed, control does not scale. Confidence does.

The most expensive thing ever managed is potential never unleashed. Every day spent controlling work others should own is a day someone else spends scaling impact still being debated.

The future belongs to those confident enough to let go of control so others can build it.

PART III The Future Is an Invitation

"The future is not some place we are going, but one we are creating.

The paths are not to be found, but made.

And the activity of making them changes both the maker and the destination."

—John Schaar, political theorist

I'm standing in line at Starbucks in San Francisco. The woman ahead orders her usual. The barista, maybe 22, suggests a new roast. She declines. She knows what she likes.

"But have you tried it?" he asks.

"I don't need to. I've been ordering the same thing for 10 years."

"Exactly," he says. "That's why you should try it."

She laughs, dismissing him. She grabs her usual and leaves.

He turns to me, shakes his head. "Ten years of the same coffee. Imagine ten years of the same anything."

That interaction is the choice everyone faces. Stick with what's known, even when it stops working. Or try something different, even without guarantee it's better.

The five cyclones aren't slowing. AI evolves faster than organizations adapt. Markets shift before strategies solidify. The next generation refuses to accept Industrial Age constraints. Everything accelerates except willingness to change.

William Gibson said it perfectly: "The future is already here—it's just not evenly distributed." Some companies, some leaders, some people are already demonstrating a future-ready mindset. Others are clinging to the Industrial Age. The future doesn't wait for even distribution. Early adopters thrive. Late movers get left behind.

Through Purpose, Exploration, Action, Collaboration, and Empowerment, successful navigation becomes possible. Control is gone forever. Prediction was always an illusion anyway. What remains is internal confidence, that doesn't need external validation.

Yet understanding the importance of P.E.A.C.E. doesn't guarantee successful transformation. Awareness of new approaches doesn't prevent reverting to old patterns when pressure mounts. Fear still surfaces because biology doesn't disappear. Control still tempts because it feels safer than trust. And over-analysis will always disguise itself as progress.

Fear isn't the problem. Pretending you're not afraid is.

P.E.A.C.E. isn't complicated. Living it is. Making it daily practice. Building environments where it becomes the natural rhythm, where organizations transform because the people inside them already have.

The barista was right. Ten years of the same anything, when everything around you changes, is stagnation.

The question isn't whether you understand P.E.A.C.E. It's whether you'll live it.

In Chapters 9 and 10, the shift becomes personal.

Chapter 9 rebuilds the internal architecture that determines whether P.E.A.C.E. becomes daily practice or good intention—shifting identity from position to purpose, learning to use fear as a navigation tool rather than a stop sign, and seeing exactly what future-ready looks like when the pressure is real.

Chapter 10 delivers the proof: P.E.A.C.E. in full motion, at scale, under conditions nobody controlled. Then comes the only question that matters. The future doesn't belong to the most experienced, the most credentialed, or the most knowledgeable.

It belongs to those who move when there is no map. Permission isn't coming.

The invitation to build the future is in your hand.

9 The Future-Ready Mindset

"Between stimulus and response there is a space.

In that space is our power to choose our response.

In our response lies our growth and our freedom."

—Viktor Frankl, psychiatrist and Holocaust survivor

That space—in which you choose your response—is where identity shifts.

When identity moves from position to purpose, from title to impact, everything changes. "I am a manager" becomes "I develop people." "I am an engineer" becomes "I solve problems through technology."

It takes brutal inner strength—to release who you've been for who you're becoming. To choose internal clarity over external approval. That's a future-ready mindset. It doesn't come easy.

The younger generation never fell into this trap. They don't introduce themselves by job title. They share what they create. Identity comes from impact, not position. They were born navigating.

The five cyclones make positional identity obsolete. Roles disappear faster than anyone can claim them. When AI can do the tasks, one question remains: what makes you irreplaceably human?

When identity shifts from external validation to internal creation, fear loses its grip. You can't lose what you are—only what you're called. You can't become obsolete when you define yourself by what you create.

Identifying Your Value

The Industrial Age turned people into human doings. Value measured by output. Worth determined by productivity. Identity defined by tasks completed. "What do you do?" became the first question, as if doing defined being.

It went deeper than identity. The Industrial Age built an entire economic model around hours worked. The more you produced, the more you earned, the more you were "worth." That created a race to produce more, earn more, buy more. It distorted how society values a person. It deepened the divide between haves and have-nots. And it accelerated the destruction of the planet through constant disposal and consumption. The cycle fed itself: work harder, buy more, throw away, repeat. That is the Industrial Age mindset at its most damaging.

Emergence exposes the lie underneath all of it. When AI can do the tasks better, faster, and cheaper, what is left? The uniquely human value. Creativity. Intuition. Connection. Purpose. Empathy. Who you actually are.

Some people think it's either AI or humans. AI wins and people become obsolete, or humans resist and stay relevant. Both are wrong.

The future is AI doing what AI does best. Crushing productivity, accessing global perspectives instantly, processing information at a speed no human can match. Meanwhile, humans do what humans do best. Understand experiential context that AI misses. Bring empathy that AI can't feel. Ask the deeper questions that AI overlooks. Collaborate with purpose. Create what has never existed.

AI makes you more productive. You make AI more effective. That's multiplication, not replacement.

The human being returns. Human doing gets amplified through technology. AI handles the repetitive. Humans reclaim their essence as creative, intuitive, connected, purposeful navigators of what comes next.

The Window That's Opening

A marketing manager who built a career on campaign creation watches AI generate stronger campaigns in seconds—and invests time in brainstorming messages for new markets. A financial analyst sees AI process data instantaneously—and redirects his focus to provide the insights only human judgment can deliver. A coder discovers AI writes cleaner code faster—and moves up the stack to solve harder problems.

These are real shifts happening now, in months, not years.

AI changes the equation through collaboration, not competition. It's $1 + 1 = 3$. Humans amplified by AI can create what neither could achieve alone. The Industrial Age served its time. Now the next paradigm is here, blending what worked with what's emerging.

The five cyclones of change are accelerating simultaneously. ChatGPT reached 100 million users in two months. Institutions that took centuries to dominate lose credibility in days. And the Human Cyclone keeps asking: what makes you irreplaceably human when machines deliver faster?

The compound effect of falling behind grows exponentially. Organizations that hesitated on digitalization for five years now need ten years to catch up. Those waiting another year may never recover. The gap between emergence thinkers and Industrial Age operators widens daily.

Leadership used to be about having answers.
Now it's about asking better questions.

Jensen Huang treats AI like a debate partner, asking the same question across multiple models, then prompting them to critique each other. I use AI the same way. Not for answers but for perspective, challenge, possibility. This is the evolution from human doing (using AI to complete tasks) back to human being (using AI to expand thinking).

AI demands more thinking, not less. The difference between people who gain real benefit and those who find it a nice add-on is whether they're assigning tasks or exploring possibilities.

The question is whether to transform by choice or by force. Adobe chose transformation and grew more than tenfold, from a $16 billion market cap to more than $250 billion at its peak.[1] BlackBerry resisted and disappeared. The window for choosing shrinks daily.

Fear as Navigation Tool

Fear arrives predictably. The moment before speaking up in a meeting. The pause before hitting "send" on the resignation letter. The hesitation before saying yes to the new opportunity. Most people interpret fear as a stop sign. In Emergence, it's navigation.

Chapter 2 revealed the biology: the amygdala firing faster than conscious thought, the substantia nigra craving familiar patterns. This wiring saved our ancestors from tigers. Now it blocks us from speaking out against norm—the same instinct based on biological response to mortal danger, yet now triggered by the idea of standing up for a new approach in a boardroom.

Fear contains information worth decoding. Not all fear is the same. Protective fear is a legitimate warning—real danger, real signal. Expansion fear is something else entirely: the sensation of standing at the edge of growth. One keeps you safe. The other keeps you small. The critical skill isn't eliminating these fears. It's learning to tell them apart.

Your body knows the difference before your brain does. Protective fear feels heavy, dark, contracting—your nervous system pulling back, energy dropping, your gut saying stop. That signal serves you. Listen to it.

Expansion fear feels electric, anticipatory, alive. The body leans forward despite the fear. Future-ready leaders learn to distinguish between the two through body intelligence and intuition.

Marie lived this distinction daily. Cycling through occupied territory triggered both fears. Protective fear told her to vary her route, watch for patrol changes, trust no one completely. Expansion fear pushed her to speak at the bridge, feed the Jewish captives, help the enemy soldiers. She used protective fear as information and expansion fear as invitation.

The pattern holds today in Emergence. Protective fear warns: this partner can't be trusted, this action risks legal exposure, this customer won't adopt. Future-ready navigators don't react to this fear. They listen, intuit, and then ask: what's the worst that can actually happen?

Expansion fear whispers: this presentation will fail, this innovation won't work, this conversation will get uncomfortable. It's lying. Take a breath and move through it.

Protective Fear. Expansion Fear. Know the Difference

During Adobe's transformation, protective fear warned about cash flow during the transition. They listened and planned carefully. Expansion fear warned about customer rejection. They moved through it and discovered customers recognized the advantages of flexible subscriptions more than costly purchases.

Rapid growth of AI triggers both fears simultaneously. Protective fear is real: some jobs will disappear, some skills will become obsolete, some companies won't survive. Plan accordingly. Expansion fear is different: I'll become dependent, I'll lose what makes me special. These fears keep you from discovering ways to use AI to amplify your unique human value.

The practice is simple. Feel fear. Go internal. Ask: is this protecting me or limiting me? If protecting, honor it. If limiting, thank it and move forward anyway.

Gen Z has a different relationship with fear because they've never known a predictable world. Fear is background noise for them, not an exceptional event. They move through expansion fear naturally because staying still feels more dangerous than moving forward.

Future-ready companies blend all generations, just as they integrate AI with human intelligence. A 60-year-old's experience combined with a 25-year-old's digital fluency, plus AI's power, creates competitive advantage far beyond what anyone could achieve alone.

Integration, not replacement, is the critical factor for future-readiness. Experience and speed. Intuition and data. Human and machine.

Stop Resolving the Tension. Use It

Future-ready leaders live in tension. They get comfortable with discomfort. The necessity to navigate without maps, to decide without certainty, to lead without knowing where the path goes. This tension is where innovation lives. Necessity is the mother of innovation. You can't remove the tension. You learn to thrive in it.

The contradictions that confuse Industrial Age thinkers become superpowers in emergence. What looks contradictory through a linear lens becomes complementary through an emergence lens.

Industrial Age mindset	→	Future-ready mindset
Control everything	→	Letting go creates alignment
More resources = better results	→	Constraints enable creativity
Avoid failure	→	Fail fast to succeed faster
Trust takes years to build	→	Confidence enables collaboration
Specialize deeply	→	Flow between capabilities
Plan then execute	→	Explore through action
Individual excellence	→	Collective capability
Protect knowledge	→	Share to amplify
Wait for certainty	→	Gain certainty through action
Learn from experts	→	Learn by experience
Manage risk	→	Embrace risk
Value money	→	Value impact

These aren't abstract philosophy. They're the operating principles of leaders who are already winning in the world that's emerging. And the shift isn't gradual—it's a threshold. Once you see through an emergence lens, the old calculations stop making sense. A new math takes over.

Leadership is a Calculation

Gianpiero Petriglieri, professor of organizational behavior at INSEAD and one of the world's top fifty management thinkers, cut through the noise at the Oslo Business Forum in 2025. Leadership, he argued, is a calculation—and the math is simple:

Hope > Fear

Work you show > Work you ask

Freedom > Demands

Greater than. Not instead of—greater than.

In every interaction, you're tipping the scale one way or the other. You're generating more hope than fear—or more fear than hope. You're leading by example, demonstrating through action—or demanding through position. You're creating freedom within boundaries—or tightening the grip.

The equation doesn't lie. And neither does your team's response to it.

Control was a leadership strategy for the Industrial Age. In emergence, control is how you fall behind.

The people navigating emergence live these equations daily. Those struggling violate them consistently. The math is simple. The discipline transforms everything.

As you use P.E.A.C.E., you will feel the tension:

- **Purpose.** Staying true to your purpose means saying no to misalignment so you can say yes to what matters. Adobe rejected easy revenue to create lasting value.
- **Exploration.** Boundaries enable discovery. Kristian's 12-month exploration gave more insight than peers' 4-year programs. Constraints force creativity that open-ended freedom rarely finds.
- **Action.** Speed improves quality. McKinsey's data validated. Fast decisions are better decisions. Tiger teams delivered results for Barloworld in months not years because momentum provided clarity.
- **Collaboration.** Competition and cooperation aren't opposites. Google and Microsoft collaborate on standards while competing on products. Strong competitors make the best partners when purpose aligns.
- **Empowerment.** Less oversight creates more alignment. Ritz-Carlton's employees make better decisions with $2,000 authority than committees make with unlimited budgets.

These aren't abstract ideas. They're operational realities. DaimlerChrysler failed because they couldn't integrate: precision engineering and innovative disruption needed to coexist, but leadership forced a choice instead of resolving the tension. They chose one and lost both. Adobe succeeded because they tackled the paradox: serve shareholders and serve customers simultaneously. They chose both and it worked.

The shift from "either/or" to "both/and" thinking is the mindset shift that emergence demands.

> Industrial Age thinking asks whether to go fast or maintain quality. Emergence thinking asks how speed can enhance quality.
>
> Industrial Age thinking asks whether to collaborate or compete. Emergence thinking explores ways collaboration strengthens competitive position.

Every leader navigating emergence faces these questions daily. The future-ready ones have stopped choosing sides.

Operating in Real Time

Industrial Age thinking is sequential. First strategy, then planning, then execution. This linear approach assumes time for each step. That time no longer exists.

Emergence happens in real time. While exploring options, you're simultaneously testing solutions. While testing, you're collaborating with partners and customers. While collaborating, you're empowering teams to iterate. All five forces of P.E.A.C.E. happening at once. Not in sequence.

Adobe's transformation demonstrated this. They didn't explore, then decide, then act. They explored subscription models by building them, collaborating with customers, and empowering support teams. Narayen didn't wait for perfect information. He orchestrated simultaneous movement toward the North Star. That was the inflection point. The moment they stopped thinking in steps and started thinking in systems.

Each element reinforces the others in real time. Purpose guides while exploration uncovers while action tests while collaboration accelerates while empowerment scales. The pattern creates momentum that sequential approaches cannot match.

People with an Industrial Age mindset are still scheduling meetings to discuss options. By the time they decide to act, emergence thinkers have already iterated three times.

The mindset shift is profound. Stop asking "What should we do first?" Start asking "What can happen simultaneously?" Stop asking "When will we know enough to act?" Start asking "What can we learn through acting?"

Technology amplifies real-time results. AI processes data while you sleep. Global teams work across time zones. Digital tools enable instant collaboration. Markets operate around the clock. Sequential thinking in a simultaneous world guarantees obsolescence.

The invitation is simple. Start something before you're ready. Learn what you need along the way. Build what doesn't exist yet. Collaborate with people you haven't met yet. Empower others to do the same. All of it, at once.

Cultivating Emergence Culture

Culture isn't what's on the wall. It's what people do, feel, and believe when no one's watching. Most companies default to what they know—programs, innovation workshops, transformation initiatives, agility courses. These fail because culture isn't programmed. It's practiced. The difference isn't semantic. It's structural.

Neuroscience explains why. Every time you pause before reacting, listen to intuition before data, go internal before going external—you're rewiring the brain. Cognitive habits migrate from the prefrontal cortex, where they require deliberate effort, to the substantia nigra, where they become instinctive. The leader who once had to remind herself to ask questions before giving answers eventually can't imagine leading any other way. That's not a mindset shift. It's a brain shift. And it's permanent.

This is why Emergence Culture can't be implemented through a quarterly initiative. It grows through five daily patterns that make P.E.A.C.E. a reflex, not a reference.

- **Intention.** Before external chaos, internal clarity. Five minutes: what's my North Star today? What needs exploration? What requires action? Not motivation. Navigation.

- **Alignment.** Before major decisions, pause. Does this serve the North Star? Is this reaction or response? What would courage look like? Three questions that shift decisions from automatic to intentional.
- **Learning.** When something fails, harvest it. What did we discover? What assumptions were wrong? How fast can we try again? Failure becomes data, not verdict.
- **Connection.** Break silos deliberately: coffee across departments, reverse mentoring across generations, leaders face-to-face with the people they serve.
- **Celebration.** Recognize emergence behaviors, not just results. The leader who killed their own project because it no longer served purpose. The team that failed fast and saved millions. Celebrate what should be repeated.

When these patterns become consistent, culture shifts without proclamation. People go internal before deciding. They explore before committing then act before certainty arrives. They collaborate across boundaries. Each moment is small, while the accumulation is transformative.

This isn't soft territory. It's strategic advantage. Organizations that cultivate Emergence Culture adapt faster, innovate more effectively, and retain the talent Industrial Age cultures quietly lose.

The Inflection Point

Emergence isn't linear progression. It's pressure building until something breaks through.

The five cyclones spin independently, but when they converge, they create inflection points: sudden shifts that change everything. Shifts that, in hindsight, could be seen coming.

COVID wasn't a random crisis. It was cyclone convergence. Global interconnection made a pandemic inevitable. Speed meant the virus outran institutions. Confidence collapsed in real time. People questioned everything about how they lived and worked. When physical connection disappeared, it forced a reckoning about what defines humanity. All five cyclones converging transformed work, education, commerce, and life itself within weeks.

ChatGPT's launch in November 2022 was another inflection point. The technology wasn't new—AI had been developing for three decades. But cyclone convergence caused eruption: 100 million users in two months. Abstract AI became concrete reality overnight. What could be trusted? What was human value worth if machines could do the work?

The cyclones are tectonic plates, pressure building through constant motion. More inflection points are coming. The next might be climate-triggered migration, a quantum computing breakthrough, or something none of us can imagine. The specific event doesn't matter. The pattern does.

You don't need to wait for an inflection point.

By embracing Emergence—looking past fear, committing to purpose, exploring, acting, collaborating, empowering—you create an inflection point inside your own organization. Delivering results without drama and making decisions without committees. Solving problems without permission.

That's contagious. Meetings become productive because someone asks "What's our purpose here?" Decisions accelerate because someone says "Let's just try it for two weeks and evaluate the results based on the agreed upon criteria." Tiger teams outperform committees, so more form. Purpose-driven projects succeed, so purpose becomes the filter.

Adobe didn't just change one company. It changed how software and value gets delivered worldwide. When enough people operate with emergence mindset, Industrial Age approaches become obviously obsolete. Emergence comes from evolution, not revolution.

The goal isn't to predict the future. It's to become the kind of leader who can navigate whatever comes next. You don't need a global inflection point to start. You are one.

When You Slip

Biology doesn't disappear because you embrace emergence. The amygdala still fires. The substantia nigra still craves familiar patterns. Under pressure, people revert to Industrial Age conditioning. This is human. Expect it.

The slip is predictable. A deadline approaches. Pressure mounts. Suddenly you're seeking approval instead of trusting judgment. Building consensus instead of making decisions. Analyzing instead of acting. Controlling instead of empowering. P.E.A.C.E. starts to evaporate under biological stress.

Recognition is the first step back. Notice the symptoms: energy dropping, creativity disappearing, everything feeling urgent but nothing feeling important. Meetings multiplying and joy evaporating. These are signs you've slipped from emergence into Industrial Age survival mode.

Going internal shows the pattern. That familiar tightness—fear and instinct running the show. That familiar exhaustion—trying to control what can't be controlled. The frustration—operating from external pressure instead of internal purpose. The body knows before the mind admits it.

Recovery isn't complicated. Stop. Breathe. Go beyond instinct to your intuition. Ask: what's my North Star? Not the deadline—but the purpose. Not the pressure—the possibility. Ten seconds of internal clarity can prevent ten hours of external chaos.

Each recovery builds resilience. The first slip might last weeks before you recognize it. The next, days. Then hours. Then minutes. The slips don't stop. Recognition accelerates and recovery strengthens.

This is where grit matters most. Not in heroic moments. In boring ones. The grit to go internal when everything screams urgency. To pause when reaction would be easier. To return to purpose when pressure pulls you away.

Adobe's leaders slipped repeatedly. Quarterly earnings triggered old patterns. Customer complaints triggered defensive responses. Competitor moves triggered reactive strategies. But each time, they returned to purpose faster. The North Star grew stronger than the biological pull. Every return was an inflection point.

Marie must have slipped countless times. Fear overwhelming purpose. Exhaustion defeating determination. The urge to quit, hide, survive instead of serve. But she got back on the bicycle every morning.

The return is the practice.

The Story Continues

Marie, whose bridge moment opened this book, didn't end her story with the war. The teenager who navigated occupied territory became a woman who navigated life with the same principles. After the war, it was no longer necessity. It was choice.

In 1948, she emigrated to America with her soldier husband and infant daughter. The cross-Atlantic journey led to a bus ride across the American desert, so foreign she said it felt like "going to another planet." Military wives at the base store mocked "that German woman." Marie didn't speak English in public for six months. She listened, learned, explored. Then one day she turned to her detractors and said in perfect English: "My English is better than your German." They apologized. She'd earned respect through patience and preparation.

When her younger sister Gertrude and boyfriend Hans asked how to emigrate to America, Marie didn't give them a plan. She said: "Think hard about why you want to come—what is the purpose. Explore your options. If it feels right, take action: get married, book passage to New York. I'll help with the rest." P.E.A.C.E. in action, before it had a name.

Gertrude and Hans arrived at Ellis Island in 1954. Marie was waiting. She helped them settle, find work, build lives—then guided three more siblings to America, each learning to navigate emergence for themselves. She didn't find them jobs, teach them English, or secure their housing. She showed them the path and stepped back. Each person she empowered went on to empower others.

In her later decades, Marie lived in Emergence. She ate when hungry. Slept when tired. Made decisions from inner knowing. The practices she'd developed under pressure became her way of being. Going internal became daily navigation, not emergency response. Purpose became contribution, not survival. Empowerment became joyful multiplication.

She lived in P.E.A.C.E. long before it had a name. She just lived it and empowered others to do the same.

After her daughter Carolyn died of cancer at 64, grief could have consumed 85-year-old Marie. Instead, she returned to her purpose: keeping people safe and warm.

She knitted. Hundreds of hats annually. Thousands over the following years. For newborns and hunters, neighbors and strangers, school teams and church groups. For five generations of family, including great-great-grandchildren not yet born.

By age 96, she had knitted more than 10,000 hats. The University of Louisville awarded her the Gold Standard of Optimal Aging for her selfless dedication to giving back.

Marie continued knitting until the day she died in February 2023. Her last hat lay half-completed on the bed beside her. Still keeping people safe and warm with her final breaths.

Her story answers the critical question: is emergence sustainable? Marie lived it for seventy years after the war. Not perfectly—she had fears, doubts, difficult days. But she never let external circumstances dictate her internal state. She never again gave away her power to navigate.

In my nightly calls during the last decade of her life, she would say: "During the war I learned I could handle anything. Through life, I learned that intuition is the only map you ever truly need."

That is the whole book in two sentences.

Today's bridge isn't concrete and steel. It's a mindset shift—Industrial Age conditioning on one side, emergence possibility on the other. Marie had no choice but courage. You have something more: conscious understanding of what you're choosing and why.

The path is clear. The choice is yours. The future is emerging.

Your Turn: Future-Ready Mindset Reflection

Living in Emergence requires intentional practice. Not complicated. Not time-consuming. Just consistent. These questions create the rhythm that makes P.E.A.C.E. sustainable.

Morning questions (2 minutes):

- What's my North Star today?
- What fear will be growth in disguise?
- Where can I release control and gain power?
- What would courage look like today?
- How will I know I'm responding, not reacting?

Midday reset (30 seconds):

- Am I creating or performing?
- What would a navigator do here?
- Is this serving purpose or just creating motion?
- Where am I overcomplicating?
- What needs to happen versus what I think should happen?

Evening integration (3 minutes):

- What did I learn about myself today?
- Where did I slip back to Industrial Age thinking?
- What emerged that I didn't expect?
- Who did I empower without realizing it?
- What would I do differently with internal confidence?

Weekly deeper reflection:

- Is my identity expanding or contracting?
- What paradox am I struggling to hold?
- Where is biology overriding consciousness?
- What pattern keeps repeating?
- How has my North Star evolved?

These are navigation tools. Some days you'll skip them. Some days you'll need them desperately. The practice isn't perfection. It's showing up. Getting it real, not getting it right.

The questions evolve as you do. What challenges beginners becomes automatic. What seems impossible becomes natural. The practice deepens not through adding complexity but through increasing honesty.

Marie didn't have formal questions, but she lived the inquiry. Each day choosing response over reaction. Each decision filtered through purpose. Each action aligned with inner knowing. The questions simply make conscious what she did by intuition.

You understand P.E.A.C.E. You've seen how others transformed through it. You know the practices that sustain it. You recognize the patterns that undermine it. You have everything needed to live in emergence.

Except one thing: the choice to begin.

10 The Invitation Awaits

"Life can only be understood backwards; but it must be lived forwards."

—Søren Kierkegaard, Danish philosopher

When COVID-19 was declared a pandemic by the World Health Organization in 2020, most people froze. I didn't.

I was fascinated. While many saw disaster, I viewed it as one of the most interesting experiments in human adaptation unfolding in real time.

Walking out of my Oslo office, through the streets, into grocery store aisles—my brain was buzzing. This massive shift was what I'd been preparing for my whole life. Not with bunkers or supplies. With mindset.

The Grocery Store Revelation

In the grocery store KIWI, I noticed Morton, the store manager, moving like a man possessed. Restocking faster than should be physically possible, talking to suppliers, making decisions simultaneously without breaking stride. He had that glint. Not stress. Not fear. Pure flow state.

(*continued*)

> (*continued*)
>
> We made eye contact across the chaos. He grinned. We both knew.
>
> "Is this like the coolest freaking thing ever?"
>
> His face lit up. "Yes! This is so bizarre!"
>
> Two emergence minds recognizing each other. While others worried about supply chains and isolation, Morton and I were fully alive—not thinking *how will I survive this?* but *WOW. Let's see what emerges.*

That's the shift from external validation to internal confidence. When I transformed Next Step years earlier, my worth wasn't tied to an office or predictable revenues. The cyclones of change didn't threaten my identity. They revealed it.

Morton's eyes in March 2020 showed the same thing—a future-ready person leaning into the cyclones instead of running from them.

April Rinne, author of *Flux* and a futurist, put it plainly at the Oslo Business Forum in 2025: "Uncertainty is opportunity in its purest form."[1] When maps fail, navigation begins.

The map is gone. Your only real advantage now is how quickly you learn while moving.

Morton and I weren't being recklessly optimistic about chaos. We were recognizing opportunity in its raw state, before it gets processed into plans and procedures.

This is an emergence mindset in its purest form. When everything changes, you come alive. You've been waiting for this. Your intuition recognizes the moment: change is where purpose becomes clear.

The Long Arc of Emergence

The world emerging today did not arrive suddenly. It has been building for more than a century.

The second Industrial Revolution, igniting in the 1880s, unleashed productivity the world had never seen. Electrification, mass manufacturing, global commerce—wealth that transformed societies. The post-World War II boom accelerated it further. The middle class expanded. Prosperity grew. Consumption grew with it.

So did the cost.

By the 1970s, the warning signs were impossible to ignore. The atmosphere was changing. Resources were depleting. The model that built prosperity was eroding the foundation it stood on.

Then the 1980s opened a different door. Technology began its exponential climb. Personal computing, the internet, mobile connectivity—each wave opened new industries, new business models, new ways of working. Minds constrained by geography suddenly had reach. The seeds of what is emerging now were planted then.

Throughout these decades, five cyclones were forming: Speed, Confidence, Meaning, Pressure, and Humanity. Most leaders experienced them as separate challenges—a technology disruption here, a workforce shift there. They managed each in isolation, reaching for Industrial Age frameworks to contain forces those frameworks were never built to handle.

The cyclones converged anyway. The internet revolution. The 2008 financial crisis. The smartphone transformation. Each was an inflection point—foreseeable in hindsight, arriving faster than the one before.

Then COVID arrived. Not just a health crisis—the inflection point that made emergence impossible to ignore. Every assumption about how work functioned, how leaders led, what mattered—exposed as fragile. The Industrial Age scaffolding, weakening for decades, cracked in full view. Eighteen months later, ChatGPT made the abstract concrete, the future present, and the optional mandatory.

The past will not, cannot, be rebuilt.

What's different now isn't Emergence itself. It's the acceleration. The interval between inflection points is shrinking. The next one is already building—and the specifics matter less than your readiness when it arrives.

The question isn't when. It's who you'll be in that moment.

Will you be panicking about what's disappearing? Or fully alive because finally something interesting is happening?

Emergence means moving with clear purpose as your North Star—exploring new paths, acting before certainty arrives, collaborating to build what no one builds alone, empowering those who follow.

The arc stretches back decades. The future begins now.

Tomorrow Morning's Choice

You don't need a global pandemic to embrace Emergence. You don't need an AI revolution to develop the mindset. Your emergence inflection point arrives daily in smaller forms.

Tomorrow morning, an email will shift your plans. A meeting will change direction. A decision will demand a response without complete information. An opportunity will appear that scares you. These are practice runs for the bigger inflection points ahead.

The question is how you'll respond. Will you react from Industrial Age conditioning, seeking approval, analyzing endlessly, protecting territory? Or will you respond from emergence, going internal for clarity, acting on purpose, collaborating across boundaries?

The shift doesn't require a dramatic declaration. It starts with one different response. When the urgent email arrives, pause before reacting. When the meeting goes sideways, ask "what's really important here?" When the opportunity scares you, notice if it's expansion fear or protective fear. When someone needs a decision, make it from internal confidence rather than external validation.

Each small choice builds the muscle for bigger ones. Each emergence response makes Industrial Age patterns feel more foreign.

I know this because I have lived it. In 2020, COVID turned a five-week business trip into a decade living in Norway. The Industrial Age playbook said panic, retrench, protect. I went internal, aligned with my purpose, and embraced the new possibilities that emerged. I have never looked back. The Emergence mindset made it navigable.

Start with What You Have

Marie didn't have a P.E.A.C.E. model to navigate occupation. Shantanu Narayen didn't build a five-year business transformation plan. They started where they were with what they had.

You have more than any of them. You understand the directions of the wind from each of the five cyclones. You are equipped with P.E.A.C.E. You've seen how others have used it to shift mindset and transform companies and industries. You recognize the patterns that trap and the practices that liberate.

But more importantly, you have today. The meetings, the emails, the decisions, the interactions. Each one is an opportunity to embrace emergence: focus on your purpose, navigate by the North Star, go internal listening to your intuition, exploring, taking action, collaborating, and empowering. Not someday. Tomorrow morning.

The Compound Effect of One

You, fully alive during Emergence, empower others without saying a word. Navigating uncertainty without panic demonstrates that following an internal compass works. Excitement about emergence shows others that it can be energizing instead of threatening.

Transformation succeeds through demonstration, not programs. When you stop seeking approval before acting, others notice. When you collaborate across boundaries, silos weaken. When you respond rather than react, the energy shifts.

At some point you'll recognize another emergence thinker across the chaos. That spark of shared understanding. That mutual excitement about what's possible. These connections form naturally, creating ecosystems of people who navigate rather than panic, who create rather than protect.

This is distributed transformation. Millions of individual choices aggregating into collective evolution. Each person practicing P.E.A.C.E. makes it easier for others to choose Emergence over Industrial Age exhaustion.

Permission Is Not Coming

Nobody authorized my response to COVID. Marie didn't wait for permission to speak up and save lives. Adobe's leaders didn't ask the market's permission to transform.

No one will tap you on the shoulder and say "you're ready." No certificate of emergence thinking exists. No committee will approve your transformation. The invitation to live differently is self-issued.

It starts with taking responsibility. Claiming your power rather than waiting for it to be granted. Starting before you're ready because ready never comes. Beginning with what you have because a clear plan forward is an Industrial Age fantasy.

The Thread That Runs Through Everything

When I talk about Adobe's transformation, people hear "boxed software to subscriptions" and think they understand it. They don't. Because the real story isn't about a business model change. It's about a thread that started in 2008 and hasn't stopped building since.

Our team was embedded from the beginning, as I described in Chapter 3. What most people get wrong comes from the surface view. The shift to Creative Cloud wasn't just moving software from a desktop to the cloud. It was a fundamental change in the relationship between Adobe and every person using their tools.

In the old world, you bought a license. Your software and files lived on your PC. If something crashed, your work could disappear. Neither Adobe nor any other provider knew what you actually did with their products.

Moving to the cloud changed everything. Cloud means storing software and data on remote servers accessed through the internet, so your tools and your work stayed in Adobe's protected environment. If you wanted a colleague in another country to see your design, you just gave them access. No file transfers, permissions, or version confusion.

But the real shift was underneath all of that. With data in the cloud, Adobe could see what people actually used. Not to monitor them. To serve them better. If designers in Spain gravitated toward certain color tools, Adobe could develop more of what they needed. If architects in Japan used specific 3D features, those features got priority improvements. Every user interaction became information that made the next experience better.

This was land and expand in action. Land and expand means attracting users with core value, then growing the relationship based on their actual behavior. Get people creating in the cloud. Learn what they love then give them more of it. The stickiness came from relevance, not lock-in.

And this is where most people's understanding stops. "Adobe went subscription. It worked. End of story." But it was actually the beginning.

All that user data flowing through the cloud made something bigger possible: use of machine learning to continually improve user experience. Through the Sensei machine learning platform, Adobe analyzed the patterns of millions of users across Creative Cloud, Document Cloud, and Experience Cloud. Long before anyone was talking about AI, Sensei was predicting what users wanted and Adobe was delivering it.

Think about that timeline. We moved the tools and data to the cloud in the early 2010s. That provided the foundation to apply machine learning through the mid-2010s. Machine learning was extended, allowing integration of AI capabilities directly into the tools people used every day. Each phase built on the last. There were no separate projects or business plans. Just one thread, building as the market and customer needs evolved.

When ChatGPT launched in late 2022 and generative AI became the world's new obsession, Adobe had a massive head start. The infrastructure was already there. The data was already flowing. The machine learning was already delivering. Adding generative AI capabilities to tools that millions already used was an acceleration, not a pivot.

Adobe wasn't the only one ahead of the curve. In 2018, Next Step was engaged to reposition the branding and go to market approach for SimplifAI, a Norwegian company delivering AI tools for insurance claim processing. Years before anyone had heard of OpenAI, they were using AI to do real document processing work. When ChatGPT was launched, SimplifAI's response was simple: the world caught up with us. Today they are market leaders in insurance GPT.

This is what Emergence looks like in practice. You can't see the full arc while you're building it. In 2008, nobody in Adobe was planning for a generative AI boom. They were navigating the necessary shift away from a business model that had made them billions. But each decision, move to cloud, learn from data, build intelligence into tools, created the foundation for what came next.

And, the thread keeps building.

The Full Circle

As of this writing, Adobe's fiscal 2025 revenue of $23.77 billion, nearly all from subscriptions, tells one story. The bigger story is what it represents—a company that learned to navigate Emergence and never stopped.

Creative Cloud democratized access to professional tools globally. Students, entrepreneurs, and creators who could never afford $2,500 boxed software now access the same capabilities for a monthly subscription. That's emergence in action: not knowing how, but knowing why—then discovering the path through exploration, action, and collaboration.

The Future Being Built Today

The thread reaches into education now. This might be where it matters most.

Adobe has rolled out AI-forward solutions to more than 150 Creative Campus university partnerships worldwide—Howard University, Indiana University, California State, UT San Antonio, Aston University, San Jose State, and growing. Next Step's most recent engagement transformed delivery of these AI-powered offerings to universities: not layering technology onto old teaching models, but enabling teachers to facilitate real learning.

Education institutions face three obstacles to AI adoption—all rooted in Industrial Age thinking. Teachers who believe their value lies in controlling access to knowledge, and fear AI will replace them. Administrators who believe AI equals plagiarism and unemployability. Students who secretly use whatever tools they choose with no guidance or guardrails.

Adobe's responsible AI solutions break down each obstacle—and the reason it works is DNA-deep. Adobe was founded on one principle: protection of intellectual property. Their cloud environment doesn't crawl the web or leave back doors open. It verifies everything. Within that protected space, professors and students can truly collaborate. Teachers engage students in building and creating—not just receiving. Students develop portfolios demonstrating real capability: podcasts, videos, interactive presentations, problem-solving in action. Experience as a person, amplified by AI, makes Creative Campus graduates more attractive to employers.

Adobe began by navigating its own emergence. Now it empowers the next generation to create within theirs.

The 49 percent of younger professionals who told the World Economic Forum there's zero value in higher education aren't wrong about the old model. Creative Campus students won't need to unlearn Industrial Age thinking. They've never been taught it. They are what success looks like when educators align with reality instead of resisting it.

AI won't replace leaders. But leaders who know how to leverage AI as they navigate forward will replace those who don't.

That choice belongs to everyone now—not just executives in boardrooms or professors in universities. Emergence doesn't wait for people to catch up or committees to approve. It is here, already at full force, indifferent to whether you are ready.

The choice was never whether to transform. It is whether you navigate intentionally toward your North Star or drift reactively, carried by forces you never chose to engage.

The future is being built right now. In organizations and on platforms, by leaders brave enough to act and empower rather than dictate, and teams open to exploration and collaboration—moving toward the North Star. By leaders willing to release control and discover what purpose-aligned people create when given space. By individuals who stopped waiting for certainty and started moving with clarity. Every step on the journey adds another future-ready navigator to a world that needs more of them urgently.

Emergence is not a future event. It is the present reality of everyone reading these words.

What started with one CEO's uncertain walk in 2008 now shapes how millions learn, create, and prepare for futures nobody can fully predict. The cyclones that seemed abstract are the air we all breathe. The inflection points that once arrived every decade now arrive every few hours. The emergence that was coming is here.

The circle isn't closing. It's expanding.

And the only question that remains is the one only you can answer: will you navigate it—or wait for someone else to draw you a map that no longer exists?

The Invitation Starts Now

You have more power to create than any generation before you. AI amplifies what you can do. Global networks put you in reach of anyone. Tools that cost millions a decade ago are free today.

The cyclones are spinning. The gap between Industrial Age thinking and emergence thinking has never been more visible. And you're standing right in the middle of it.

That's not a burden. It's a gift.

You could have been born in an era of predictable routine, where maps worked and following the rules guaranteed success.

Instead, you're here. Now. When purpose matters more than position and one person with the right idea can reshape an industry.

You may have been born in an era of predictable routine, where maps worked and following the rules guaranteed success.

Now, you're here. Right now, when purpose matters more than position and one person with the right idea can reshape an industry.

Tomorrow morning, the same circumstances look different. The chaos that exhausts others becomes energy. The uncertainty that paralyzes others becomes invitation.

This is your moment.

Epilogue

What a Time to Be Alive

The five cyclones won't slow. Emergence will accelerate. The next inflection point is already building. That next wave that changes everything overnight.

But you're no longer waiting for predictability that won't return. You have what Marie had at that bridge: internal clarity about what matters and courage to act on it. Plus something she didn't have: P.E.A.C.E. as a navigation system for continuous emergence.

P.E.A.C.E. provides your navigation system for continuous emergence. Purpose points the way. The rest builds the momentum to get there.

The choice Marie faced at the bridge is the choice facing you tomorrow morning. Let fear decide what happens next, or act on what you know to be true. The Industrial Age conditioning will pull you toward reaction, approval-seeking, analysis. The emergence mindset will pull you toward purpose, intuition, action. You already know which one serves you.

Future-ready navigators aren't waiting. They're already building the future while committees debate what it should look like. They understand what Marie knew by intuition: in emergence, those who act with purpose while others hesitate don't just survive. They define what's possible.

Marie lived to 97, navigating Emergence by choice for nearly eight decades after the war. Her final hat lay half-completed beside her.

The question isn't whether you can navigate emergence. Marie proved humans can. The question is whether you'll wait for crisis to force evolution, or choose it now while you still have the option.

Don't wait for your bridge moment. Every day offers smaller ones. Choices between reaction and response. Between fear and purpose. Start now.

Fear is optional. Emergence is inevitable.
What a time to be alive.

Keep Navigating

This book began with Marie on a bridge in Ampfing, Germany—a 19-year-old navigating impossible conditions with a clarity that came from absolute internal knowing, long before anyone had a name for what she was doing.

She wasn't extraordinary because she was fearless. She was extraordinary because she acted anyway.

Marie went on to navigate nearly eight more decades of emergence—immigration, loss, reinvention, joy—always returning to the same five words that anchored her purpose: *keep people safe and warm*. In her final years, she channeled that purpose into knitting. More than 10,000 hats. For newborns and strangers, for grandchildren and great-great-grandchildren not yet born.

She knitted until the day she died at 97 in February 2023. Her last hat lay half-finished on the bed beside her.

Marie is my aunt. This book is her story as much as mine.

She never read a leadership framework. She never attended a transformation workshop. She just lived P.E.A.C.E.—for more than 90 years—because she understood something most leaders spend careers trying to learn: the map doesn't disappear when conditions change. You become the map.

Her bridge is yours now. You know what to do.

Join the Journey into the Future

The ideas in this book don't live on the page. They live in the decisions you make tomorrow morning, in the meetings where fear masquerades as caution, and in the moments when emergence shows up before you feel ready.

Journey Into the Future is the global community where future-ready leaders keep that momentum alive—sharing real-world lessons, challenging each other's thinking, and co-creating what comes next. Not a webinar or podcast series of experts talking. A community of practitioners who have chosen emergence over extinction.

Join us on jennifervessels.com/journey-into-the-future

Bring Emergence to Your Organization

Reading sparks the mindset. The work ignites it.

My keynotes, executive retreats, and leadership workshops bring these stories, approaches and tools into the room—live, practical, and built on the same two decades of Fortune 100 transformation behind this book. Not theoretical slides. Not someone else's story borrowed for the occasion. Your people leave equipped and committed to act—because they've experienced what future-ready leadership actually feels like.

Adobe. Cisco. Novartis. IKEA. Google. Microsoft. The concepts in this book were forged in the real work of transforming organizations that couldn't afford to get it wrong. That's what I bring to every stage and every session.

If you're building a leadership event, executive offsite, or transformation initiative and want a partner who delivers results—not just inspiration—I'd welcome a conversation.

Jennifer@JenniferVessels.com
www.JenniferVessels.com
linkedin.com/in/jennifervessels

Appendix

Navigating AI with P.E.A.C.E.

The 70 percent to 90 percent failure rate for AI initiatives isn't a technology problem. It's a navigation problem. The technology works. People simply start wrong: with the tool instead of the problem, with the rollout instead of the test, with the mandate instead of the purpose.

AI amplifies everything, including mistakes. Leaders rushing to "implement AI" without clear navigation create expensive failures. Those who wait for perfect conditions create a different kind of failure—obsolescence.

If your strategy for AI is "wait for a policy," you've already fallen years behind your competitors.

My aunt, Marie, had no policy. Standing at that bridge in Ampfing in 1945, she did have purpose—she knew what outcome she needed. She had the willingness to test her assumptions in real time. And she had the confidence to act before the path was clear.

Eighty-five years later, the future-ready leaders who are succeeding with AI today are doing the same thing.

They are applying P.E.A.C.E. to the specific challenge of AI adoption. This works because AI is emergence—continuous, accelerating, and indifferent to whether you're ready or not.

Purpose: Start with the Problem, Not the Technology

Most AI initiatives fail at this first step. They start with "We need an AI strategy" or "Everyone's using ChatGPT so we should too." That's technology-first thinking, which is expensive and fails.

Start with a Specific Business Problem

When Schneider Electric came to Next Step struggling with fragmented data across global business units, they wanted a tool to "do AI on our data." We stopped that conversation and asked a different question first: what specific decision is being delayed right now because people don't have enough complete information? That reframe changed everything.

We led their tiger team's exploration of alternative tools, applying one, checking in with other departments to validate the results, then they empowered the full business unit to roll out the AI-amplified data analysis solution.

It delivered measurable results in weeks—because it was built around a real problem, not a technology trend.

Start with a specific business problem. It should be clear, measurable, and easily recognizable to the stakeholders in one department or business unit.

Wrong Versus Right Questions

WRONG: "How can we best use AI?"
RIGHT: "How do we consolidate accurate financial reports from 15 subsidiaries across 25 countries within 48 hours?"
WRONG: "We need to implement AI to speed customer response."
RIGHT: "How do we reduce the time our processors spend on basic claims so they can focus on complex cases requiring human judgment?"

Define Success Criteria Before You Start

The purpose isn't "use AI." The purpose is solving a real problem. Write down, before exploring any tools, what success looks like. Be ruthlessly specific—vague success criteria guarantee failure.

- **Accuracy of AI-generated results.** Must be 85%+ accurate on first pass.
- **Usability.** Mid-level team members can use it without extensive onboarding.
- **Speed.** Reduces time from 45 minutes to under 10 minutes.
- **Innovation.** Generates or sparks brainstorming to generate new ideas.
- **Integration.** Works with our existing systems without major overhaul.

Be ruthlessly specific. Vague success criteria ("more efficient," "better results") guarantee failure.

Exploration: Test Multiple Tools, Not Just One

Here's where most organizations waste millions: they pick one AI tool based on vendor presentations, then try to make it work for everything. Explore at least three different AI tools that address similar requirements—not to pick the "best" one, but to understand what trade-offs each makes.

Why three minimum?

Two creates binary thinking, this one OR that one. Three (or more) forces nuanced understanding, what does each prioritize? What does each sacrifice? Under what conditions does each excel?

The Multi-Tool Testing Process

1. Select two to three AI tools that can potentially address your specific problem: different generative AI models (Claude, ChatGPT, Gemini), specialized AI tools for your industry, or different approaches (predictive AI, analysis AI, automation AI).
2. Test each with the same problem for one to two weeks maximum. Use actual data—not hypothetical scenarios. Have the people experiencing the problem do the testing, not IT, not consultants. Document what works, what doesn't, what surprises you.
3. Compare results against your success criteria defined in Purpose. Which met accuracy requirements? Which was actually usable by your team? Where did results differ, and why?

> **The Jensen Huang Method**
>
> NVIDIA's CEO Jensen Huang doesn't rely on a single AI tool for any important question. He uses multiple generative AI systems, asks each the same question, then critically analyzes why the answers differ. This practice—interrogating the gaps between outputs—is how NVIDIA maintains competitive intelligence at scale while avoiding the blind spots that sink single-source AI adoption. When NVIDIA's teams began applying this multi-tool approach systematically, they found that approximately 30 percent of questions yielded meaningfully different answers depending on the tool—differences that would have been invisible, and potentially costly, if they'd used only one source.

Critical Thinking Is Nonnegotiable

Don't just accept AI outputs—interrogate them. Ask: what assumptions does this response make? What perspectives does it exclude? What would change if the framing changed?

Effective AI use takes *more* critical thinking, not less, because you're evaluating machine logic rather than human judgment. That's brain-intensive work. It takes more time than not using AI. But it produces better results than blindly trusting one tool's output.

Context, Specificity, and Guardrails

Good AI results come down to three things:

- **Context** means telling AI what you're actually trying to achieve. Don't just ask "what goes in mushroom soup." Tell it: I'm serving a small, light mushroom soup as an appetizer before lamb chops for six guests. Give it the North Star.
- **Specificity** means saying exactly what you mean. Twenty years ago I asked my admin Jean to "book a meeting, 10 to 11." At ten minutes before eleven, five people showed up. Jean had booked the meeting at 10:50. That was my mistake, not hers. The same applies to AI—imprecision in, imprecision out.

- **Guardrails** mean stating the criteria: gluten free, light, a precursor to lamb. With guardrails, you get a precisely calibrated answer. Without them, you get slop.

Action: Small Tests with Clear Metrics

Once exploration shows which tool(s) directly address your specific problem, take action. Start small with implementation within one team, business unit, set of data for a defined period, one to three weeks maximum.

The instinct at this stage is to go big—enterprise-wide rollout, annual contracts, elaborate infrastructure, a freshly minted "center of excellence." Resist every one of those impulses. They signal commitment before learning, which is the most expensive mistake in AI adoption.

Instead, define boundaries and take action deliberately: one specific problem, a small tiger team of four to eight people, a defined time period of one to three weeks—no longer.

Your success metrics are already written; you defined them when aligning on the Purpose of the initiative. Highlight them to all on the team. At the end of the action period, evaluate against those criteria with a yes or no verdict. Not sort of. Not it could if we . . . Either the tool solved the problem or it didn't.

Example: Financial Consolidation Pilot

Problem: Consolidating financial reports from multiple subsidiaries

Tool Selected: AI tool specifically for financial data integration.

Action: Test with two subsidiaries (Malaysia and South Africa) for two weeks.

Success Metrics: 85%+ accuracy rate; usable by two mid-level accounting staff; 60%+ reduction in consolidation time; no major IT infrastructure changes required.

At the end of the action period, evaluate against the criteria you defined in Purpose. Yes or no. Be clear—did this use of AI solve the problem or not?

If yes → Move to Collaboration. If no → Return to Exploration with a different tool or revised criteria.

Be honest about failure. Most AI implementations fail because people commit too much before learning what actually works. Small actions let you fail fast and cheap—not slow and expensive.

Collaboration: Create Guidelines, Not Mandates

AI implementation fails when IT builds it in isolation, then hands it to the business. It succeeds when the people experiencing the problem shape how the solution works.

Form a tiger team that will take exploration deeper, challenge one another, share learnings along the journey. It should be a small group (five to eight people) including:

- People experiencing the business problem.
- One person with AI technical knowledge (not to lead, to support).
- Someone from IT (to drive integration needs).
- A skeptic (someone who questions whether AI is the right approach).

Not committees. Not departments. Small, focused teams with the problem. Adobe's transformation demonstrated this at scale: their tiger teams consistently achieved in two months what traditional committees had failed to produce in eighteen.

Develop AI Guidelines Collaboratively

All organizations and future-ready navigators today need AI guidelines, policy or requirements to provide clear guardrails.

These are written, documented rules and agreements made by all regarding use of AI. This is not IT-created policy handed down. It must be developed *with* the people who will use the tools.

Guardrails need to include specifically the tools that are approved, types of data that are approved for sharing with an AI, output review requirements and guidelines such as:

- **What types of problems should AI be considered for?**
  - Repetitive tasks or data processing → Yes
  - Complex judgment calls → No

  - High-volume pattern recognition → Yes
  - Sensitive customer complaints → Requires human review
  - Data tracking and analysis → Yes
  - Predictions of trends, behaviors, opportunity → Yes with people
  - Generation of code, tools, materials, documents → Yes with people
- **How do we verify AI outputs?**
  - Financial data → Spot check 10 percent against source
  - Customer communications → Human review before sending
  - Internal reports → Compare against previous patterns
  - Creative work → Team review for brand consistency
- **When do humans get involved?**
  - AI confidence score below 80 percent → Human review required
  - Customer escalation → Immediate human involvement
  - Unusual patterns → Flag for human analysis
  - High-stakes decisions → AI informs, humans decide
  - Sensitive topics, requirements or multicultural tasks → Human led
- **How do we measure ongoing success?**
  - Check accuracy weekly and monthly against success criteria
  - Discuss with team members, customers, partners, suppliers: how has your experience of interaction with us changed in the past weeks, months?
  - Monitor for drift: is AI performance declining?
  - Review every quarter: what should we continue, modify, or stop?

AI capabilities and risks are emerging daily. The guardrails you put in place must evolve through collaboration. What works for the finance team might not work for operations. What saves time for the team may not improve the customer relationship. The people doing or who are impacted by the work understand the real results. The guidelines must emerge based on their perspective.

Empowerment: Give People Boundaries, Then Trust Them

When you have guidelines in place, are clear on the purpose of AI—that is, the problems to be solved and the success criteria are clear—empower people to use AI within the guardrails.

This means:

DO empower people to

- Use AI for problems that fit within the guardrails
- Explore different tools and approaches within the boundaries
- Suggest improvements to guidelines based on experience
- Think critically when reviewing all outputs from AI
- Collaborate openly, sharing learnings, concerns, and new approaches
- Use AI to amplify their success as a human

DON'T

- Require approval for every AI use
- Create elaborate permission structures
- Mandate AI use in areas in which human skills are critical
- Assume initial guidelines are permanent

Monitor through metrics, not micromanagement

Every two to four weeks, check:

- Are success criteria still being met?
- Has accuracy/speed/usability declined?
- Are people finding new valuable uses?
- Are guidelines being followed?

If metrics decline

- Bring tiger team back together
- Diagnose: tool changed? Problem changed? People using it wrong?
- Adjust guidelines or tool selection as needed

If new uses emerge

- Document what's working
- Update guidelines to include valuable new applications
- Share learnings across organization

> ***The fishing rod principle:** You don't solve problems for people with AI. You empower them to solve problems themselves using AI as a tool. They need to understand how to use it, when to trust it, and when to question it.*
>
> *If you do the work for them, they stay dependent. If you empower them with clear boundaries and trust, they become more capable.*

The Critical Difference: Brain-Intensive Work

Throughout all five phases, remember: **effective AI use takes *more* time and *more* brain power than not using AI.**

AI handles routine work, the tasks our brain's substantia nigra does on autopilot. But using AI effectively demands intensive engagement from the prefrontal cortex, the parts that think critically, synthesize information, question assumptions.

When you effectively use AI, you:

- Test multiple tools and sources, not trust one output
- Compare results and analyze differences
- Question why AI reached specific conclusions
- Verify outputs against reality
- Think more deeply about what actually matters

That's not "doing more with less." That's doing more important work because AI handles less important work.

The promise that AI creates efficiency is true, but only if you invest the cognitive effort to use it intelligently. Leaders who treat AI as a shortcut get shortcut results. The ones who treat AI as a tool enabling deeper thinking get transformational results.

Common Failures to Avoid

These are common failures to avoid:

Failure mode	What to do instead
Starting with technology instead of problem	"We need to implement ChatGPT" wastes money. "We need to reduce contract review time from 3 days to 3 hours" gets results.
Testing only one tool	Single-source AI creates single-perspective thinking. Multiple tools reveal trade-offs and limitations.
Rolling out before learning	Enterprise-wide implementations before small tests guarantee expensive failures.
IT-driven instead of business-driven	The people experiencing the problem must shape the solution. IT advises; business leads.
Ignoring human factors	If people don't trust it, don't understand it, or don't see value, the best AI sits unused.
Assuming "set it and forget it"	AI tools evolve. Problems change. Guidelines require regular review and adjustment.
Measuring activity instead of outcomes	"We implemented AI" means nothing. "We reduced error rates by 40 percent" means everything.

The 90-Day Quick Start

P.E.A.C.E. is not theory. It is a sequence of deliberate actions, each one building on the last. The guide below translates that sequence into a 90-day sprint—structured enough to move with clarity, constrained enough to learn without overcommitting. Thirteen weeks. Five elements. One specific problem to start. That is all this requires.

Weeks 1–2: Purpose

- Identify one specific business problem
- Define clear success criteria
- Get buy-in from people experiencing the problem

Weeks 3–6: Exploration

- Select three to four potential AI tools
- Test each for one week with real problem
- Compare results against success criteria

Weeks 7–8: Action

- Run small pilot (5–10 people, 2 weeks)
- Measure against success criteria
- Decide: continue, adjust, or stop

Weeks 9–10: Collaboration

- Form tiger team
- Develop AI use guidelines collaboratively
- Document what works, what doesn't

Weeks 11–12: Empowerment

- Expand to broader team within guidelines
- Set up metric monitoring (monthly checks)
- Create feedback mechanism for improvements

Week 13+: Iterate

- Review metrics monthly
- Adjust guidelines as needed
- Apply learnings to next problem

It's about learning how to navigate AI through bounded action. When you've done it successfully once, you understand the pattern for expanding.

Remember: AI Is Emergence in Action

Everything in this book about navigating emergence applies to AI adoption:

- You can't plan perfectly before starting
- It's not AI or humans—it's people amplified by effective use of AI
- Internal confidence matters more than external certainty
- Small actions with clear boundaries beat big transformations
- The people experiencing the problem have essential insight
- Guidelines evolve through experience, not theory

AI won't slow down. It won't wait for perfect strategies or complete readiness. Future-ready navigators are embracing AI-amplified emergence.

They are moving forward, learning through action, adjusting based on experience with P.E.A.C.E.

Purpose. Exploration. Action. Collaboration. Empowerment. You already know how to do this. The question is when you'll start.

That's not a rhetorical flourish. After 20 years transforming Adobe, Cisco, IKEA, Novartis, and dozens of others, I can tell you with certainty: the leaders who succeed at the inflection point aren't the ones who had better information. They're the ones who moved first, with purpose, while others were still debating whether the bridge was safe to cross.

Marie didn't cross that bridge because she had a plan. She crossed it because her purpose was clear and her fear was optional.

The same P.E.A.C.E. that carried a 19-year-old across a wartime bridge in Ampfing carries leaders across the AI inflection point today. Not because the methodology is magic—but because purpose, exploration, action, collaboration, and empowerment are what humans do when they decide to show up for what's next rather than defend what's past.

The map hasn't disappeared. You are the map.

But maps don't navigate themselves.

Start now. The future isn't waiting—and neither are the leaders already building it.

Notes

Introduction

1. John B. Furness "The Enteric Nervous System and Neurogastroenterology." *Nature Reviews Gastroenterology & Hepatology* 9 (2012):286–294.
2. J. Andrew Armour, "Anatomy and Function of the Intrathoracic Neurons Regulating the Mammalian Heart," in *Reflex Control of the Circulation*, ed. Irving H. Zucker and Joseph P. Gilmore (Boca Raton, FL: CRC Press, 1991). Also: HeartMath Institute, "Heart-Brain Communication," *Science of the Heart*, https://www.heartmath.org/research/science-of-the-heart/heart-brain-communication/.

Part I

1. Tim Ferriss. "Reed Hastings, Co-Founder of Netflix—How to Cultivate High Performance, the Art of Farming for Dissent, Favorite Failures, and More (#730)." *The Blog of Author Tim Ferriss*, April 3, 2024. https://tim.blog/2024/04/03/reed-hastings/.
2. Jeff Galvin, Laura LaBerge, and Evan Williams. "The New Digital Edge: Rethinking Strategy for the Postpandemic Era." *McKinsey Digital*, May 26, 2021. https://www.mckinsey.com/capabilities/mckinsey-digital/our-insights/the-new-digital-edge-rethinking-strategy-for-the-post pandemic-era.

3. McKinsey & Company "What Is Digital Transformation?," McKinsey Featured Insights, updated August 2024. https://www.mckinsey.com/featured-insights/mckinsey-explainers/what-is-digital-transformation.
4. Gartner, cited in multiple industry analyses including Statista, "Digital Transformation—Statistics and Facts," updated 2024, https://www.statista.com/topics/6778/digital-transformation/. The figure reflects organizations with at least one active digital initiative.
5. Eric Lamarre, Kate Smaje, and Rodney Zemmel, *Rewired: The McKinsey Guide to Outcompeting in the Age of Digital and AI* (Hoboken, NJ: Wiley, 2023). Digital savviness data from Michael Schrage, Benjamin Pring, David Kiron, and Desmond Dickerson, "Leadership's Digital Transformation: Leading Purposefully in an Era of Context Collapse," MIT Sloan Management Review, January 26, 2021, https://sloanreview.mit.edu/projects/leaderships-digital-transformation/.

Chapter 1

1. Visual Capitalist, "How Long Does It Take to Hit 50 Million Users?," Visual Capitalist, June 8, 2018, https://www.visualcapitalist.com/how-long-does-it-take-to-hit-50-million-users/. ChatGPT figure from UBS, "Let Me ChatGPT That for You," UBS Global Research, February 1, 2023, citing data from Similarweb.
2. Scott D. Anthony, S. Patrick Viguerie, Evan I. Schwartz, and John Van Landeghem, "2021 Corporate Longevity Forecast," Innosight, 2021, https://www.innosight.com/insight/creative-destruction/.
3. R. B. Fuller, *Critical Path* (New York: St. Martin's Press, 1981). IBM projection cited in David Russell Schilling, "Knowledge Doubling Every 12 Months, Soon to be Every 12 Hours," Industry Tap, April 19, 2013, https://www.industrytap.com/knowledge-doubling-every-12-months-soon-to-be-every-12-hours/3950.
4. Pew Research Center, "Public Trust in Government: 1958–2025," December 4, 2025, https://www.pewresearch.org/politics/2025/12/04/public-trust-in-government-1958-2025/. Media trust: Gallup, "Americans' Trust in Media Remains at Trend Low," October 2024, https://news.gallup.com/poll/651977/americans-trust-media-remains-trend-low.aspx.

5. Pew Research Center, "How Americans Get News on TikTok, X, Facebook and Instagram," June 12, 2024, https://www.pewresearch.org/journalism/2024/06/12/how-americans-get-news-on-tiktok-x-facebook-and-instagram/. Influencer trust data from Matter Communications, "The Relatability Report," 2023, cited in Shopify, "Influencer Marketing Statistics," 2024.
6. Triple-A, "The State of Cryptocurrency Ownership Worldwide in 2024," 2024, https://www.triple-a.io/blog/crypto-ownership-report, GitHub, "Octoverse 2024," October 2024, https://github.blog/news-insights/octoverse/octoverse-2024/.
7. Deloitte, "2024 Gen Z and Millennial Survey," May 2024, https://www.deloitte.com/global/en/about/press-room/deloitte-2024-gen-z-and-millennial-survey.html. US Bureau of Labor Statistics, "Employee Tenure in 2024," September 26, 2024, https://www.bls.gov/news.release/tenure.nr0.htm.
8. Chief Executives for Corporate Purpose, "Giving in Numbers: 2025 Edition," October 2025. Nielsen, "The Sustainability Imperative," October 12, 2015, https://www.prnewswire.com/news-releases/consumer-goods-brands-that-demonstrate-commitment-to-sustainability-outperform-those-that-dont-300157905.html. Edelman, "2025 Trust Barometer," January 2025, https://www.edelman.com/trust-barometer.
9. Gallup, "State of the Global Workplace: 2025 Report," April 2025, https://www.gallup.com/workplace/349484/state-of-the-global-workplace.aspx. Corporate Leadership Council (Gartner), "Driving Performance and Retention Through Employee Engagement," 2004, as cited in Gallup research.
10. United Nations Office for Disaster Risk Reduction, *The Human Cost of Disasters 2000–2019* (Geneva: UNDRR, 2020). World Meteorological Organization, *State of the Global Climate 2023* (Geneva: WMO, 2024). United Nations High Commissioner for Refugees, "Frequently Asked Questions on Climate Change and Disaster Displacement," https://www.unhcr.org/us/news/stories/frequently-asked-questions-climate-change-and-disaster-displacement.
11. International Monetary Fund, "*Global Debt Monitor 2025*," September 2025, https://www.imf.org/external/datamapper/GDD/2025%20Global%

20Debt%20Monitor.pdf. Institute of International Finance, "Global Debt Monitor," February 2025. McKinsey & Company, "Overcoming Global Supply Chain Challenges," April 2022, https://www.mckinsey.com/industries/logistics/our-insights/overcoming-global-supply-chain-challenges.

12. International Resource Panel, United Nations Environment Programme. *Global Resources Outlook 2024: Bend the Trend: Pathways to a Liveable Planet as Resource Use Spikes.* (Nairobi: UNEP, 2024), https://www.unep.org/resources/Global-Resource-Outlook-2024.

13. World Health Organization, "COVID-19 Pandemic Triggers 25% Increase in Prevalence of Anxiety and Depression Worldwide," March 2, 2022, https://www.who.int/news/item/02-03-2022-covid-19-pandemic-triggers-25-increase-in-prevalence-of-anxiety-and-depression-worldwide. Gallup, "Employee Burnout: Causes and Cures," 2020, https://www.gallup.com/workplace/288539/employee-burnout-biggest-myth.aspx. Centers for Disease Control and Prevention, "Youth Risk Behavior Survey Data Summary and Trends Report: 2013-2023," August 2024.

14. Stanford University, Institute for Human-Centered AI, *Artificial Intelligence Index Report 2024* (Stanford, CA: Stanford University, April 2024). Joseph Briggs and Devesh Kodnani, "The Potentially Large Effects of Artificial Intelligence on Economic Growth," Goldman Sachs Economic Research, March 26, 2023. McKinsey & Company, "*The State of AI in Early 2024: Gen AI Adoption Spikes and Starts to Generate Value*," May 2024.

15. World Economic Forum, *Future of Jobs Report 2023* (Geneva: World Economic Forum, May 2023), chap. 4.

16. US Bureau of Labor Statistics, "Number of Jobs, Labor Market Experience, Marital Status, and Health for Those Born 1957-1964," News Release, August 2023, https://www.bls.gov/news.release/pdf/nlsoy.pdf. Bankrate, "*Side Hustles Survey*," 2024.

17. Robin Dunbar, "How Many Friends Can You Really Have?," *IEEE Spectrum*, November 28, 2022. Richard Weissbourd et al., *Loneliness in America: How the Pandemic Has Deepened an Epidemic of Loneliness and What We Can Do About It* (Cambridge, MA: Making Caring Common, Harvard Graduate School of Education, February 2021). US Department of Health and Human Services, "Our Epidemic of Loneliness and

Isolation: The U.S. Surgeon General's Advisory on the Healing Effects of Social Connection and Community," 2023.

18. United Nations, Department of Economic and Social Affairs, *World Population Prospects 2024* (New York: United Nations, 2024). Pew Research Center, "Defining Generations: Where Millennials End and Generation Z Begins," January 17, 2019.

Chapter 2

1. Daniel Kahneman, *Thinking, Fast and Slow* (New York: Farrar, Straus and Giroux, 2011), 19–30.
2. Daniel Kahneman, *Thinking, Fast and Slow* (New York: Farrar, Straus and Giroux, 2011), 79–96. See also Amy F. T. Arnsten, "Stress Signalling Pathways That Impair Prefrontal Cortex Structure and Function," *Nature Reviews Neuroscience* 10, no. 6 (June 2009): 410–422.
3. M. Gawdat. *Solve for Happy: Engineer Your Path to Joy*. New York: Gallery Books, 2018.

Chapter 3

1. Deloitte. *2024 Gen Z and Millennial Survey*. Deloitte, 2024. https://www.deloitte.com/global/en/issues/work/content/genz-millennialsurvey.html.

Part II

1. For Jobs's navigation of the digital music transition and Apple's broader transformation, see Walter Isaacson, *Steve Jobs* (New York: Simon & Schuster, 2011).

Chapter 4

1. Dan Raviv, *Comic Wars: How Two Tycoons Battled Over the Marvel Comics Empire—And Both Lost* (New York: Broadway Books, 2002).
2. Sean Howe, *Marvel Comics: The Untold Story* (New York: Harper, 2012). See also Ben Fritz, *The Big Picture: The Fight for the Future of Movies* (New York: Houghton Mifflin Harcourt, 2018), 37–62.
3. Fritz, *The Big Picture*, 63–89.

4. The Walt Disney Company, "The Walt Disney Company to Acquire Marvel Entertainment for $4 Billion," Press Release, August 31, 2009.
5. Yahoo Finance, "Adobe Inc. (ADBE) Historical Prices, 2012–2024," accessed February 4, 2026.
6. Market capitalization data from CompaniesMarketCap.com. Adobe's market cap was approximately $17 billion in March 2012 when Creative Cloud was announced, growing to over $300 billion at its peak—roughly 18 times its pre-Cloud value.
7. Robert Iger, *The Ride of a Lifetime: Lessons Learned from 15 Years as CEO of the Walt Disney Company* (New York: Random House, 2019). The advice originated from a friend and political consultant who told Iger during his CEO interview preparation: "You only get three." Iger's three priorities—invest in high-quality branded content, embrace technology, and grow globally—guided Disney throughout his tenure.
8. Gartner, Inc., "Gartner Says Worldwide AI Spending Will Total $1.5 Trillion in 2025," press release, September 17, 2025. See also Stanford University Human-Centered Artificial Intelligence, *AI Index Report 2025* (Stanford, CA: Stanford HAI, 2025).
9. RAND Corporation, *Understanding the Risks and Challenges of AI Project Failure* (Santa Monica, CA: RAND, 2024). See also Gartner, Inc., "Gartner Survey Finds Generative AI Is Now the Most Frequently Deployed AI Solution in Organizations," Press Release, May 7, 2024 (finding only 48 percent of AI projects reach production). BCG, "AI Adoption in 2024: 74% of Companies Struggle to Achieve and Scale Value," October 24, 2024.

Chapter 5

1. Hannah Nordhaus, "What the 'Trash Heap' Penguins of Argentina Are Teaching Us about Survival." *National Geographic*, April 17, 2025. https://www.nationalgeographic.com/animals/article/penguins-argentina-trash-evolution.
2. Alexandra Stolba, "IKEA's Failure and Success on the Japanese Market" (bachelor's thesis, Vienna, 2013). See also "Once More With Feeling: The Story of IKEA in Japan," SME Japan, January 30, 2019.
3. "IKEA's Triumph in Japan: Unraveling the Success Story," Covue Blog, March 3, 2025. See also IKEA entry in Wikipedia, citing franchise

arrangement in 1974 and withdrawal in 1986 due to failure to adapt store layout and product dimensions.

4. "IKEA's Localization Strategy: A Masterclass in Global Expansion," Accelingo, January 17, 2024.
5. Beth Kowitt, "It's Ikea's World. We Just Live in It," Fortune, March 10, 2015. The Gwangmyeong store, IKEA's largest by shopping area at the time, was "on track to become one of Ikea's top-performing outlets for 2015."
6. Carlos A. Gomez-Uribe and Neil Hunt, "The Netflix Recommender System: Algorithms, Business Value, and Innovation," *ACM Transactions on Management Information Systems* 6, no. 4 (December 2015): 1–19. https://doi.org/10.1145/2843948.
7. Gibson Biddle, "How to Define Your Product Strategy" (essay series), Medium, 2018–2020. https://gibsonbiddle.medium.com/intro-to-product-strategy-60bdf72b17e3. Biddle was VP of Product at Netflix from 2005 to 2010.
8. Ashok Chandrashekar, Fernando Amat, Justin Basilico, and Tony Jebara, "Artwork Personalization at Netflix," Netflix Technology Blog, December 7, 2017. https://netflixtechblog.com/artwork-personalization-c589f074ad76.
9. The 80 percent figure is widely cited and originates from Netflix's own reporting. See also Gomez-Uribe and Hunt (2015), which details how recommendation improvements are measured against member retention as the primary metric.
10. Jensen Huang, interview by Fareed Zakaria, *Fareed Zakaria GPS*, CNN, aired July 13, 2025. Huang described asking the same question of multiple AIs and having them "compare each other's notes" to find the best answer, comparing the practice to seeking "three doctors' opinions."
11. Lauren Goode, "Nvidia's Hardware Is Eating the World," *Wired*, February 23, 2024. In this interview Huang confirmed using Perplexity AI and ChatGPT "almost every day" for research. See also Jensen Huang, remarks at the World Economic Forum, Davos, January 21, 2025, in which he referenced ChatGPT, Gemini, and Claude by name.
12. Jessica Stillman, "Steal Nvidia CEO Jensen Huang's 1 Simple Trick to Get the Best Answers from AI," *Inc.*, August 4, 2025.

Chapter 6

1. "The Rise and Fall (and Rise Again?) of BlackBerry," Harvard Digital Innovation and Transformation, 2018. https://d3.harvard.edu/platform-digit/submission/the-rise-and-fall-and-rise-again-of-blackberry/.
2. Statista, "The Terminal Decline of BlackBerry," based on Gartner data, accessed February 4, 2026. https://www.statista.com/chart/8180/blackberrys-smartphone-market-share/.
3. Gartner, quarterly smartphone market share reports, 2007–2016. Stock price data from Nasdaq historical records. BlackBerry's all-time high closing price was $147.55 on June 19, 2008. See also "A Brief History of Research In Motion," InvestorPlace, January 2013. https://investorplace.com/2013/01/a-brief-history-of-research-in-motion/.
4. Charles Arthur, "RIM Chiefs Mike Lazaridis and Jim Balsillie's Best Quotes," The Guardian, June 29, 2012.
5. [1] Emily Rella, "93% of Gen Z Use Two or More AI Tools Per Week, Google Survey Finds," Entrepreneur, November 25, 2024. Based on a Google Workspace survey of Gen Z knowledge workers. [2] Deloitte, "Global 2024 Gen Z and Millennial Survey," May 2024. Based on 22,841 respondents across 44 countries. https://www.deloitte.com/global/en/about/press-room/deloitte-2024-gen-z-and-millennial-survey.html.
6. Jennifer Vessels, "How Fragile is Agile: The Key to Making Change," keynote at the 31st Annual EuroFinance International Treasury Management Conference, Messe Wien Exhibition & Congress Center, Vienna, September 21–23, 2022.
7. Eric Ries, *The Lean Startup: How Today's Entrepreneurs Use Continuous Innovation to Create Radically Successful Businesses* (New York: Crown Business, 2011). Ries defines MVP as the version of a new product that allows a team to collect the maximum amount of validated learning with the least effort.
8. Iskandar Aminov, Aaron De Smet, Gregor Jost, and David Mendelsohn, "Effective Decision Making in the Age of Urgency," McKinsey & Company, April 30, 2019. Based on a McKinsey Global Survey of 1,259 participants. The "twice as likely" finding applies specifically to big-bet

and cross-cutting decisions. https://www.mckinsey.com/capabilities/people-and-organizational-performance/our-insights/decision-making-in-the-age-of-urgency.

9. Simon Sinek, in conversation at Virgin StartUp, October 2020. Sinek told a similar version of this story in his remarks on "Building High-Performing Teams" at Oslo Business Forum, September 24–25, 2025. At OBF, Sinek emphasized that leaders fail when "they think they have to do it all alone" and urged leaders to "share the burden and ask for help, especially from your team."

Chapter 7

1. "Daimler-Benz Announces Purchase of Chrysler Corp.," History.com, updated May 7, 2024, https://www.history.com/this-day-in-history/may-7/daimler-benz-announces-purchase-of-chrysler-corp. The equity value of $36 billion made it the largest acquisition by a foreign buyer of a US company at that time.
2. "Cerberus to Take Over Majority Interest in Chrysler," DaimlerChrysler press release, May 14, 2007. Cerberus acquired 80.1 percent of Chrysler for $7.4 billion (€5.5 billion). NBC News reported that Daimler "actually paid a dowry to unload Chrysler," injecting more than the sale price to cover restructuring costs.
3. For Schrempp's role in engineering the original merger, see Jürgen Grässlin, *Jürgen Schrempp and the Making of an Auto Dynasty* (New York: McGraw-Hill, 2000). For a critical account of the merger's failure, see Bill Vlasic and Bradley A. Stertz, *Taken for a Ride: How Daimler-Benz Drove Off with Chrysler* (New York: William Morrow, 2000).
4. Google, "Guide: Understand Team Effectiveness," re:Work, accessed February 5, 2026, https://rework.withgoogle.com/guides/understanding-team-effectiveness/. Based on Project Aristotle (2012–2014), which studied more than 180 Google teams. See also Charles Duhigg, "What Google Learned from Its Quest to Build the Perfect Team," *New York Times Magazine*, February 25, 2016.

5. Mitel, "Mitel Completes Acquisition of ShoreTel," press release, September 25, 2017, https://www.mitel.com/about/newsroom/press-releases/mitel-completes-acquisition-of-shoretel. Enterprise value approximately $430 million; equity value approximately $530 million. Synergy Research Q2 2017 UCaaS Market Share Report confirmed number two global position.
6. "1975 Icelandic Women's Strike," Wikipedia, last modified February 2026, https://en.wikipedia.org/wiki/1975_Icelandic_women%27s_strike. See also Kvennasögusafn Íslands (Women's History Archives of Iceland) and the documentary *The Day Iceland Stood Still*, directed by Pamela Hogan (2024).
7. "Halla Tómasdóttir," Office of the President of Iceland, accessed February 4, 2026, https://www.forseti.is/en/the-president/. Tómasdóttir was elected on June 1, 2024, and took office on August 1, 2024, as Iceland's seventh president and second woman to hold the office.
8. The term was coined by Ray Noorda, founder of Novell, and developed into a strategic framework by Adam M. Brandenburger and Barry J. Nalebuff, *Co-opetition* (New York: Currency Doubleday, 1996). Examples of tech industry co-opetition include the US AI Safety Institute Consortium (2024), which includes Apple, Google, OpenAI, Meta, and over 200 other entities collaborating on AI safety standards while competing intensely in AI products and services.
9. Erik Larson, "Hacking Diversity with Inclusive Decision Making," Cloverpop, September 2017, https://www.cloverpop.com/blog/research-shows-diversity-inclusion-better-decision-making-at-work. Based on analysis of 566 business decisions made by 184 teams. Teams in general outperform individuals 66 percent of the time. Teams diverse in gender, age, and geography outperform individuals 87 percent of the time.
10. Sundiatu Dixon-Fyle, Kevin Dolan, Vivian Hunt, and Sara Prince, "Diversity Wins: How Inclusion Matters," McKinsey & Company, May 19, 2020. Based on analysis of more than 1,000 large companies across 15 countries. Finding measures top-quartile vs. bottom-quartile ethnic/cultural diversity on executive teams. McKinsey notes correlation, not causation.

11. Institute for Corporate Productivity (i4cp). Cited in multiple Deloitte and industry analyses.
12. Corel Corporation (operating as Alludo), "Collaboration Survey," published June 7, 2022, via Globe Newswire. Survey found 64 percent of employees reported poor collaboration costing 3–5 hours of productivity per week.

Chapter 8

1. Joseph A. Michelli, *The New Gold Standard: 5 Leadership Principles for Creating a Legendary Customer Experience Courtesy of the Ritz-Carlton Hotel Company* (New York: McGraw-Hill, 2008). Ritz-Carlton co-founder Horst Schulze established the policy. Employees rarely spend anywhere near the $2,000 limit. The real value, as Ritz-Carlton leadership describes it, is the freedom to act.
2. Vas Narasimhan introduced "inspired, curious, and unbossed" as Novartis's cultural framework when he became CEO in 2018, shifting the company from a top-down management model to one where leaders act as servant leaders and employees are empowered to bring ideas forward. Vas Narasimhan, interview by David Rubenstein, *The David Rubenstein Show: Peer-to-Peer Conversations*, Bloomberg Television, recorded February 15, 2024.
3. US Bureau of Labor Statistics, "Employee Tenure in 2024," news release USDL-24-1971, September 26, 2024, https://www.bls.gov/news.release/tenure.nr0.htm. Based on January 2024 Current Population Survey. The 25–34 age bracket in 2024 includes both Millennials and the oldest Gen Z workers. Overall median tenure across all workers fell to 3.9 years, the lowest since 2002.

Chapter 9

1. Adobe Inc. (ADBE), historical stock price data, MacroTrends, accessed February 5, 2026, https://www.macrotrends.net/stocks/charts/ADBE/adobe/stock-price-history; all-time closing high of $688.37 recorded November 19, 2021, per TradingView, https://www.tradingview.com/symbols/NASDAQ-ADBE/.

Chapter 10

1. April Rinne, keynote address, Oslo Business Forum 2025: The Big Shift, Lillestrøm, Norway, September 24–25, 2025. Rinne is the author of *Flux: 8 Superpowers for Thriving in Constant Change* (Oakland: Berrett-Koehler, 2021). The quote also appears in the OBF post-event recap, "The Big Shift: 11 Leadership Learnings from OBF 2025," Oslo Business Forum, October 1, 2025, https://www.obforum.com/article/11-leadership-learnings-from-oslo-business-forum-2025.

About the Author

Jennifer Vessels doesn't just talk about the future of business, she builds it. As CEO of Next Step, she has spent more than two decades driving transformation for the world's most influential organizations, including Adobe, Cisco, Google, IKEA, Microsoft, and Novartis. Operating between Silicon Valley and Europe, Jennifer translates cutting-edge technology and emerging workforce dynamics into actions that deliver measurable results.

Her work spans business model shifts, AI integration, digital strategy, and organizational agility, often delivered simultaneously. Jennifer's experience empowering people to navigate through converging, accelerating forces revealed the gap this book addresses: leaders don't need another change management framework. They need proven tools they can confidently use when the map disappears mid-journey.

The power of P.E.A.C.E.—Purpose, Exploration, Action, Collaboration, Empowerment—emerged through Jennifer's transformation work in the early 2000s. It has since guided thousands of leaders inside Fortune 100 companies worldwide, proving equally powerful whether the disruption is technological, generational, or existential.

A sought-after keynote speaker and workshop facilitator, Jennifer is known for her bold, high-energy style and her refusal to mistake comfort for progress. She holds an MBA from San José State University, studied occupational psychology at the University of London, and achieved board certification from INSEAD. She divides her time between Silicon Valley and Oslo, Norway.

Index